Learn Thai

Through Stories, Grammar & Exercises
Book 1

by Karine Jones
Illustrated by Jessica Emmett

Thai language consultant: Onanong Wongprasert

Kawee Publishing.

For my son

Acknowledgment

I am very grateful to the people who have supported me over the past two years to make this book happen. Special thanks to Jess, my illustrator, who worked tirelessly and made this book lively and fun. I admire her professionalism and her uncompromising approach to details. To my Thai language teacher, Kwang, for reviewing this book to ensure that both the Thai language and culture were accurately represented. To my husband Ian, for always supporting and believing in me. Lastly, to my son, Alec (Kawee), who inspired me to write this book and of whom I am so proud.

Learn Thai - Through Stories, Grammar & Exercises - Book 1
By Karine Jones

Copyright © 2013 Karine Jones
First published 2013
ISBN 978-0-9575469-0-5

Published by Kawee Publishing
Website: kaweepublishing.com
Email: info@kaweepublishing.com

A catalogue record for this book is available from the British Library.

Author: Karine Jones
Illustration & Typeset: Jessica Emmett
Thai Language Consultant: Onanong Wongprasert

Printed and bound by CPI Group (UK) Ltd, Croydon CR0 4YY, United Kingdom

Contents

Introduction

For many years I searched, without success, for a language book in order to teach Thai to my young son. While I did find many such books for adults, written in Romanized Thai, only flash cards and a couple of pictionaries were available for children. To make matters worse, none included grammar or even exercises. The only Thai language books for children I could find were written in Thai script. Although I agree with the use of Thai script for learning the Thai language, it is not always practical.

Two years ago, I decided to write my own book. The stories and exercises have been beautifully illustrated by Jessica Emmett. My Thai language teacher, Kwang (Onanong Wongprasert), provided me with invaluable advice on the Thai language and culture. One of the characters has been named after her.

I have decided not to use the standard phonetic transliteration symbols because I found them very difficult for young readers. Instead, I use the Roman alphabet, as illustrated in the Guide to Pronunciation (p.6).

Also, I have included Thai script in the dialogues, vocabularies and exercises because it is much easier for native Thai speakers to read Thai script than Romanized Thai. For the non Thai speakers among you who manage to read Thai script, I have put spaces between the words to facilitate reading. Normally, there is no space between words written in Thai script.

I hope that you will enjoy this book, whether you are adoptive parents eager to teach Thai to your child/children, expats moving to Thailand wanting to learn the language, or you just love Thailand and want to get more out of your visit by communicating in Thai.

I would love to receive your feedback! Please email me at: info@kaweepublishing.com

Kawee   Kwang   Tom   Kataleeya   Phloi

How to use this book

Each lesson tells a story using the Thai vocabulary which you will find useful in everyday situations.

Read the picture scripts and try to understand as much as possible by yourself. Then, refer to the story translation. Repeat the sentences as often as possible using role play with your tutor, parents or other students. Ideally, you should practice the lessons with a Thai speaker in order to correctly pronounce the words.

For each lesson, the new words are listed under Vocabulary. The keywords are illustrated to facilitate memorization. The other new words are listed separately. Read the vocabulary several times and test your memory. If you forget the meaning of words from previous lessons, you can easily find them in the Glossary (p.81).

Each lesson includes easy to understand grammar and language notes. Understanding the grammar rules will make it easier to learn Thai. For more details, please refer to the Grammar and Language Notes (p.73).

Once you have become familiar with the new vocabulary and grammar, practice your comprehension by completing the exercises. Try to do them more than once by answering the questions on a separate sheet of paper. Some lessons include a game for one or more players. These games are an enjoyable way of practicing to speak Thai and creating sentences.

After every three lessons, there are revision exercises. It is a good idea to review the vocabulary and grammar notes before completing these exercises.

Each exercise has a key symbol which is linked to the appropriate learning skill:

Writing

Puzzle

Verbal

Art

Game

For all exercises, you can check your answers in Keys to Exercises (p.84).

Guide to Pronunciation

The phonetic transliteration used in this book has been simplified for young readers. Vowel sounds are expressed by regular vowels rather than phonetic symbols. If you do not have access to a Thai teacher/tutor, I would highly recommend verifying the pronunciation of the vowels through any good, free Thai language website. Most Thai vowels have a short and long sound. Below is a list of letters with a guide to how to pronounce each one:

Short vowels			Long vowels		
Sounds	English sounds	Thai words	Sounds	English sounds	Thai words
a	m**u**m	jà จะ will	**aa**	f**a**ther	hâa ห้า five
i	s**i**p	sìp สิบ ten	**ee**	m**ee**t	sèe สี่ four
eu	Montreux*	nèung หนึ่ง one	**euu**	Montreux* (but longer)	keuu คือ to be
u	b**oo**k	kun คุณ you	**uu**	t**wo**	nguu งู snake
e	m**e**t	dèk เด็ก child	**eh**	M**ay**	lêhk เลข number
ae	**air**	láe และ and	**aae**	**air** (but longer)	bpaaet แปด eight
o	g**o** (but shorter)	pǒm ผม I (male)	**oh**	g**o** (but longer)	ta-gohn ตะโกน to shout
au	t**o**p	ngau เงาะ rambutan	**or**	s**aw**	din-sǒr ดินสอ pencil
ua	b**oo**k + **a**	**	**uua**	t**wo** + **a**	kropkruua ครอบครัว family
ia	n**ea**r	**	**eea**	n**ea**r (but longer)	reean เรียน to study
eua	Montreux* + **a**	**	**euua**	Montreux* + **a** (but longer)	reuua เรือ boat
er	numb**er**	**	**err**	s**ir** (a bit longer)	Derrn เดิน to walk

* There is no equivalent sound in English. It is close to the French sound "eu" as in heureux (happy), or Montreux (the Swiss town).
** These vowels are rare and not used in this book.

Other vowel sounds		
am	**um**brella	nám น้ำ water
ai	**Thai**	bpai ไป to go
ao	**ou**t	kǎo เขา he/they

Thai is a tonal language which presents challenges for non-native Thai speakers. Below is a list of the five tones used in Thai transliteration:

Tone	Tone mark	Example	Guide
Mid	None	keuu (คือ) = to be	Normal voice.
Low	`	sèe (สี่) = four	Lower than normal voice.
Falling	^	hâa (ห้า) = five	The voice rises then falls sharply.
High	´	nám (น้ำ) = water	Higher than normal voice.
Rising	ˇ	kǎo (เขา) = he/they	The voice starts low then rises sharply like a question.

Lesson 1 - Making New Friends
Bòttêe 1 - Rúu jàk pêuuan mài
บทที่ ๑ – รู้จัก เพื่อน ใหม่

In this lesson, the student will learn the following:

- Greetings
- Introducing yourself
- Polite particles
- Thank you

Story - Making New Friends
Rúu jàk pêuuan mài • รู้จัก เพื่อน ใหม่

It is the first day at an international school in Bangkok.
Time to meet new friends!

Story Translation
Bòd plaae • บท แปล

(1)

Kawee: Sà-wàtdee **kráp**.   Hello.
สวัสดี ครับ

Tom: Sà-wàtdee **kráp**.   Hello.
สวัสดี ครับ

Kwang: Sà-wàtdee **ka**.   Hello.
สวัสดี ค่ะ

(2)

Kawee: **Pǒm** chêuu Kawee **kráp**.   My name is Kawee.
ผม ชื่อ กวี ครับ

Kun chêuu a-rai **kráp**?   What is your name?
คุณ ชื่อ อะไร ครับ

(3)

Kwang: **Chǎn** chêuu Kwang **ka**.   My name is Kwang.
ฉัน ชื่อ กวาง ค่ะ

Tom: **Pǒm** chêuu Tom **kráp**.   My name is Tom.
ผม ชื่อ ทอม ครับ

(4)

Kawee: Sa-baai dee mái **kráp**?   How are you?
สบาย ดี ไหม ครับ

(5)

Kwang: Sa-baai dee **ka**.   I am fine.
สบาย ดี ค่ะ

Kun là **ká**?   And you?
คุณ ล่ะ คะ

(6)

Kawee
& Tom: Sa-baai dee **kráp**.   I am fine.
สบาย ดี ครับ

Korpkun **kráp**.   Thank you.
ขอบคุณ ครับ

Vocabulary
Kamsàp • คำศัพท์

Sà-wàtdee	สวัสดี	Hello/Goodbye
Ka	ค่ะ	Polite Article (female speaker)
Kráp	ครับ	Polite Article (male speaker)
Pǒm	ผม	I (male speaker)
Chǎn	ฉัน	I (female speaker)
Kun	คุณ	You
Chêuu	ชื่อ	Name
Mái	ไหม	Question word
A-rai	อะไร	What
Sa-baai dee	สบาย ดี	To be fine
...Là?	ล่ะ	What about....?
Korpkun	ขอบคุณ	Thank you

Grammar and language notes
Waiya gawn gàp paa-sǎa • ไวยากรณ์ กับ ภาษา

kráp & pǒm

To be polite, boys end their sentences with the word "**kráp**" ครับ.

Boys use "**pǒm**" ผม to say "**I**".

ka & chǎn

To be polite, girls end their sentences with the word "**ka**" ค่ะ.

Girls use "**chǎn**" ฉัน to say "**I**".

mái

When asking a question*, the word "**mái**" ไหม is placed at the end of sentences to form yes/no questions.

Example:
Sa-baai dee **mái** kráp?
สบาย ดี ไหม ครับ

How are you?
(Literally: Are you well?)

* See Grammar and Language Notes for more details on **how to ask questions** (p. 73)

Exercises
Baaep-fèuk-hàt • แบบ ฝึก หัด

A ✏️ Complete the sentences by choosing a word from the boxes.

1. Sà-wàtdee ___ka___ (girl)   สวัสดี ค่ะ

2. Pǒm _____ Tom kráp   ผม ชื่อ ทอม ครับ

3. Chǎn chêuu Kwang _____   ฉัน ชื่อ กวาง ค่ะ

4. Sa-baai dee _____ ká?   สบาย ดี ไหม คะ

5. Sà-wàtdee _____ (boy)   สวัสดี ครับ

6. _____ chêuu Kwang ka   ฉัน ชื่อ กวาง ค่ะ

ka ค่ะ	kráp ครับ
chêuu ชื่อ	mái ไหม
chǎn ฉัน	ka ค่ะ

B 🧩 Match and link the Thai words with the English words.

Sà-wàtdee ka
สวัสดี ค่ะ
1

Pǒm chêuu Tom kráp
ผม ชื่อ ทอม ครับ
2

Kun chêuu a-rai ká
คุณ ชื่อ อะไร คะ
3

Korpkun ka
ขอบคุณ ค่ะ
4

Kun là ká
คุณ ล่ะ คะ
5

Chǎn chêuu Kwang ka
ฉัน ชื่อ กวาง ค่ะ
6

A My name is Kwang

B Thank you

C Hello

D My name is Tom

E What is your name?

F And you?

C 👄 Let's practice! Your turn to introduce yourself to your friend(s).

Say in Thai what your name is, ask someone what his/her name is and ask how the person is doing.

D ✏️ Translate into Thai.

1. Hello. _____

2. What is your name? _____

3. My name is Kawee. _____

4. How are you? _____

5. I am fine. And you? _____

E 🧩 Find and circle the words in the grid.

1. A-rai — อะไร
2. Kun — คุณ
3. Korpkun — ขอบคุณ
4. Sà-wàtdee — สวัสดี
5. Chăn — ฉัน
6. Pŏm — ผม
7. Là — ล่ะ
8. Chêuu — ชื่อ
9. Ka — ค่ะ
10. Kráp — ครับ
11. Mái — ไหม

P	C	V	T	I	Y	C	H	A	N
O	A	D	K	A	T	L	R	R	V
M	R	L	V	R	C	E	F	K	P
X	S	A	W	A	T	D	E	E	X
M	F	J	P	I	R	Z	Q	P	D
L	X	U	K	O	R	P	K	U	N
B	K	P	M	I	U	N	E	F	H
F	R	J	K	S	C	H	E	U	U
M	A	I	U	X	P	S	H	B	E
W	P	X	N	G	E	I	A	U	P

Did you know...?

Thai Nicknames

Most Thai people have a family name, a first name and a nickname (chêuu lên ชื่อ เล่น). The first name will be used officially (including school) and can be preceded by the polite article "kun" (คุณ). The nickname is given by the parents or other family members and will be used throughout the person's life. In order not to draw the attention of bad spirits, some nicknames are unflattering. Nicknames can be based on a colour, fruit, size, animal or number.

Lesson 2 - My Family
Bòttêe 2 - Kropkruua kǒng chǎn
บทที่ ๒ – ครอบครัว ของ ฉัน

In this lesson, the student will learn the following:

- Names of family members
- This/That
- Who
- Together
- How to answer a question

Story - My Family
Kropkruua kǒng chǎn • ครอบครัว ของ ฉัน

Kwang has invited her new friends Kawee and Kataleeya to a family picnic in Lumphini Park.

1
Kun mâae ka, kun pô ka, nêe keuu pêuuan ka, Kawee gàp Kataleeya ka.
Sà-wàtdee ka.
Sà-wàtdee kráp.

2
Nân keuu krai ká?
Nân keuu kun yaay gàp kun dtaa ka.

3
Nân keuu krai kráp?
Nân keuu nóng săao gàp pêe chaay ka.

4
Yàak lên dûay gan mái ká?
Yàak ka!
Yàak kráp!

5
Sànuk kráp! Sànuk ka!
Sànuk mái kráp, dèk dèk?

Story Translation
Bòd plaae • บท แปล

① Kwang: **Kun mâae** ka, **kun pô** ka, nêe keuu pêuuan ka, Kawee gàp Kataleeya ka.
คุณ แม่ ค่ะ คุณ พ่อ ค่ะ นี่ คือ เพื่อน ค่ะ กวี กับ แคทลียา ค่ะ

Mum, **Dad**, these are my friends Kawee and Kataleeya.

Kataleeya: Sà-wàtdee ka.
สวัสดี ค่ะ

Hello.

Kawee: Sà-wàtdee kráp.
สวัสดี ครับ

Hello.

② Kataleeya: Nân keuu **krai** ká?
นั่น คือ ใคร คะ

Who is that?

Kwang: Nân keuu **kun yaay** gàp **kun dtaa** ka.
นั่น คือ คุณ ยาย กับ คุณ ตา ค่ะ

That is my **grandmother** and my **grandfather**.

③ Kawee: Nân keuu **krai** kráp?
นั่น คือ ใคร ครับ

Who is that?

Kwang: Nân keuu **nóng săo** gàp **pêe chaay** ka.
นั่น คือ น้องสาว กับ พี่ชาย ค่ะ

That is my **little sister** and my **big brother**.

④ Kwang: Yàak lên dûay gan mái ká?
อยาก เล่น ด้วยกัน ไหม คะ

Do you want to play together?

Kataleeya: Yàak ka!
อยาก ค่ะ

Yes!

Kawee: Yàak kráp!
อยาก ครับ

Yes!

⑤ Kwang's dad: **Sànuk** mái kráp, dèk dèk?
สนุก ไหม ครับ เด็ก ๆ

Are you having **fun**, children?

Kawee: **Sànuk** kráp!
สนุก ครับ

Yes!

Kwang & Kataleeya: **Sànuk** ka!
สนุก ค่ะ

Yes!

Vocabulary
Kamsàp • คำศัพท์

Words for grandparents, uncles and aunts change depending on whether they are from your mother's side or father's side.

Kun dtaa
คุณ ตา
Grandfather

Kun yaay
คุณ ยาย
Grandmother

Kun bpùu
คุณ ปู่
Grandfather

Kun yâa
คุณ ย่า
Grandmother

Kun mâae
คุณ แม่
Mother

Kun pô
คุณ พ่อ
Father

Nóng săao
น้องสาว
Little sister

Kwang

Pêe chaay
พี่ชาย
Big brother

Kropkruua	ครอบครัว	Family
Nêe	นี่	This
Nân	นั่น	That
Keuu	คือ	To be
Kun	คุณ	A person
Pêuuan	เพื่อน	Friend
Gàp	กับ	And
Sànuk	สนุก	Having fun
Krai	ใคร	Who
Yàak	อยาก	To want
Lên	เล่น	To play
Dûay gan	ด้วย กัน	Together
Dèk	เด็ก	Child
Dèk dèk	เด็กๆ	Children

See Grammar and Language Notes for more details on the verb **to be** (p.76) and **dûay gan** (p.80).

Grammar and language notes
Waiya gawn gàp paa-săa • ไวยากรณ์ กับ ภาษา

yes To say "**yes**" in Thai, you sometimes just repeat the verb.

> **Yàak** lên dûay gan mái ká?
> Do you want to play together?
>
> **Yàak** kráp!
> **Yes**! ("want!")

Note: The personal pronouns (I, you, she, he, we) can often be omitted in Thai if the context is clear enough.

plural nouns In some cases, you can double a noun to show plural.

> Dèk   Child
> Dèk dèk   Children

kun To be more polite, you can add the word "**kun**" in front of mother or father or someone's name.

> **Kun** mâae   mother
> **Kun** pô   father

krai The word "**krai**" means "**who**".

> Nân keuu **krai** ká?   **Who** is that?
> Nêe keuu **krai** ká?   **Who** is this?

See Grammar and Language Notes for more details on **krai** (p.73) and **plural nouns** (p.79).

Exercises
Baaep-fèuk-hàt • แบบ ฝึก หัด

A ✏️ Does the picture match the description underneath? Tick yes or no.

1.

Nêe keuu kun pô
นี่ คือ คุณ พ่อ

☐ Yes
☐ No

2.

Nêe keuu kun mâae
นี่ คือ คุณ แม่

☐ Yes
☐ No

3.

Nêe keuu kun dtaa
นี่ คือ คุณ ตา

☐ Yes
☐ No

4.

Nêe keuu nóng săao
นี่ คือ น้องสาว

☐ Yes
☐ No

B 🧩 Match and link the Thai words with the English words.

Nân keuu krai ká?
นั่น คือ ใคร คะ **1**

A This is my grandfather.

Sànuk mái ká?
สนุก ไหม คะ **2**

B Grandmother

Nân keuu kun dtaa.
นั่น คือ คุณ ตา **3**

C Little sister

Kun yaay
คุณ ยาย **4**

D Who is that?

Nóng săao
น้องสาว **5**

E This is my dad.

Nêe keuu kun pô.
นี่ คือ คุณ พ่อ **6**

F Are you having fun?

C ✏️ Translate into Thai.

1. Who is this?   _____

2. Are you having fun?   _____

3. This is my mum.   _____

4. Grandfather (both sides of the family) _____

5. This is my big brother.   _____

6. Kataleeya and Kwang play together. _____

D ✏️ Complete the sentences by choosing a word from the boxes.

1. Sànuk _____ kráp?   สนุก ไหม ครับ

2. Nân keuu _____ ká?   นั่น คือ ใคร คะ

3. Nêe _____ pêuuan ka.   นี่ คือ เพื่อน ค่ะ

4. Nân keuu kun mâae _____ kun pô.
   นั่น คือ คุณ แม่ กับ คุณ พ่อ

5. Kwang gàp Kawee _____ dûay gan.
   กวาง กับ กวี เล่น ด้วยกัน

lên เล่น	krai ใคร
keuu คือ	mái ไหม
	gàp กับ

E 🎨 ✏️ Draw your family and write their relationship to you.

Draw pictures of your family members and in Thai write their relationship to you underneath the drawing, e.g. kun mâae, kun pô, etc.

_____

_____

_____

_____

_____

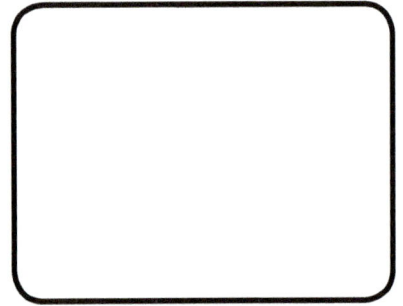
_____

Did you know...?

Fun

SÀNUK สนุก means **FUN**.
It is a very important word in Thailand. In Thai culture, there should be an element of sànuk in everyday life, even when studying or doing homework!

Lesson 3 - Discovering Bangkok
Bòttêe 3 - Tôrng Krungtêp
บทที่ ๓ – ท่อง กรุงเทพ

In this lesson, the student will learn the following:

- Methods of transportation
- To be
- Where
- To go
- By

It is the weekend. Our friends are having fun in Bangkok with their families.

1

Bpai têe Wat Phra Kâew kráp.

Bpai têe năi kráp?

Kawee bpai têe Wat Phra Kâew doy rót túk túk.

2

Rao yùu têe năi ká?

Rao yùu têe Wat Àrun ka.

Kataleeya bpai têe Wat Àrun doy reuua.

3

Sà-thănee tòr bpai Jà-tù-jàk.

Tom bpai têe tàlàat nát Jà-tù-jàk doy rót faifáa.

4

Jòrt têe nêe kráp.

Rao yùu têe Săo Ching Cháa láaew ka.

Phloi bpai têe Săo Ching Cháa doy rót taxi.

5

Kun pô, rao jà bpai têe năi ká?

Rao jà derrn bpai têe Yao-wá-ràat kráp.

Kwang derrn bpai têe Yao-wá-ràat.

6

Pŏm nèuuay jing jing!

Glàp bâahn gan tè kráp.

Kawee glàp bâahn doy rót meh.

Story Translation
Bòd plaae • บท แปล

1

Tuk tuk driver: Bpai **têe năi** kráp?
ไป ที่ ไหน ครับ

Where are you going?

Kawee: Bpai têe Wat Phra Kâew kráp.
ไป ที่ วัด พระ แก้ว ครับ

To Wat Phra Kâew please.

Kawee **bpai têe** Wat Phra Kâew **doy** rót túk túk.
กวี ไป ที่ วัด พระ แก้ว โดย รถ ตุ๊กตุ๊ก

Kawee **goes to** Wat Phra Kâew **by** tuk tuk*.

2

Kataleeya: Rao yùu **têe năi** ká?
เรา อยู่ ที่ ไหน คะ

Where are we?

Kataleeya's mum: Rao yùu têe Wat Àrun ka.
เรา อยู่ ที่ วัด อรุณ ค่ะ

We are at the Temple of Dawn.

Kataleeya **bpai têe** Wat Àrun **doy** reuua.
แคทลียา ไป ที่ วัด อรุณ โดย เรือ

Kataleeya **goes to** the Temple of Dawn **by** boat.

3

BTS** speakers: Sà-thănee tòr bpai Jà-tù-jàk.
สถานี ต่อ ไป จตุจักร

Next station is Jatujak.

Tom **bpai têe** tàlàat nát Jà-tù-jàk **doy** rót faifáa.
ทอม ไป ที่ ตลาด นัด จตุจักร โดย รถ ไฟฟ้า

Tom **goes to** Jatujak market **by** BTS**.

4

Phloi's dad: Jòrt têe nêe kráp.
จอด ที่ นี่ ครับ

Stop here please.

Phloi: Rao yùu têe Săo Ching Cháa láaew ka.
เรา อยู่ ที่ เสา ชิง ช้า แล้ว ค่ะ

We are at the Giant Swing.

Phloi **bpai têe** Săo Ching Cháa **doy** rót taxi.
พลอย ไป ที่ เสา ชิง ช้า โดย รถ แท็กซี่

Phloi **goes to** the Giant Swing by taxi.

5

Kwang: Kun pô, rao jà bpai **têe năi** ká?
คุณ พ่อ เรา จะ ไป ที่ ไหน คะ

Dad, **where** are we going?

Kwang's dad: Rao jà derrn bpai têe Yao-wá-ràat kráp.
เรา จะ เดิน ไป ที่ เยาวราช ครับ

We are walking to China Town.

Kwang **derrn bpai têe** Yao-wá-ràat.
กวาง เดิน ไป ที่ เยาวราช

Kwang **walks to** China Town.

6

Kawee: Pŏm nèuuay jing jing!
ผม เหนื่อย จริงๆ

I am really tired!

Kawee's dad: Glàp bâahn gan tè kráp.
กลับ บ้าน กัน เถอะ ครับ

Let's go back home.

Kawee **glàp** bâahn **doy** rót meh.
กวี กลับ บ้าน โดย รถ เมล์

Kawee **goes back** home **by** bus.

* Wat Phra Kâew is part of the Grand Palace compound.
** BTS, also known as BTS Skytrain, is a network of electric trains that runs throughout Bangkok.

Vocabulary
Kamsàp • คำศัพท์

Rót yon
รถ ยนต์
Car

Rót túk túk
รถ ตุ๊กตุ๊ก
Tuk tuk

Rót faifáa
รถ ไฟฟ้า
Electric train

Reuua
เรือ
Boat

Derrn
เดิน
Walking

Krêuang bin
เครื่อง บิน
Airplane

Rót meh
รถ เมล์
Bus

Rót taxi
รถ แท็กซี่
Taxi

Jàkgrayaan
จักรยาน
Bicycle

Rót jàkgrayaan yòn
รถ จักรยาน ยนต์
Motorcycle

Rao	เรา	We*	Tòr	ต่อ	Next
Jà	จะ	Will (future tense)	Tàlàat	ตลาด	Market
Gan tè	กัน เถอะ	Let's...*	Jòrt	จอด	Stop
Têe nǎi	ที่ ไหน	Where	Têe nêe	ที่ นี่	Here
Bpai	ไป	To Go	Glàp	กลับ	Go back/return
Têe	ที่	At/To	Bâahn	บ้าน	House/home
Doy	โดย	By	Derrn bpai	เดิน ไป	Go walking
Wat	วัด	Temple	Nèuuay	เหนื่อย	Tired
Yùu	อยู่	To be	Jing jing	จริงๆ	Really
Sà-thǎnee	สถานี	Station			

*See Grammar and Language Notes for more details on **personal pronouns** (p.75) and **gan tè** (p.77).

Grammar and language notes
Waiya gawn gàp paa-sǎa • ไวยากรณ์ กับ ภาษา

têe nǎi) The word "**têe nǎi**" means "**where**".

> Rao yùu **têe nǎi** ká? **Where** are we?
> Bpai **têe nǎi** kráp? **Where** are you going?

yùu) The verb "**to be**" can be expressed by "**yùu**" in order to describe being physically in a certain location.

> Rao **yùu** têe Wat Àrun ka.
> We **are** at Wat Àrun.
>
> Kawee **yùu** nǎi hôrng reean.
> Kawee **is** in the classroom

See Grammar and Language Notes for more details on the verbs **to be** and **bpai** (p.76), **têe nǎi** and **doy** (p.74).

bpai) The verb "**to go**" can be expressed by "**bpai**".

> Rao **bpai** lên. We **go** play.
>
> **Bpai** têe Sǎo Ching Cháa.
> **Go** to the Giant Swing.

doy) The word "**by**" can be expressed by "**doy**".

> Kwang bpai têe wat **doy** reuua.
> Kwang goes to the temple **by** boat.
>
> Kawee bpai têe wat **doy** rót meh.
> Kawee goes to the temple **by** bus.

Exercises
Baaep-fèuk-hàt • แบบ ฝึก หัด

A    Translate into Thai.

1. Kawee goes home by tuk tuk. _____

2. We are at Jatujak market. _____

3. Kwang goes to the market by bus. _____

4. Where are we? _____

5. Where are we going? _____

6. We are walking home. _____

B    Complete the crossword using the picture clues.

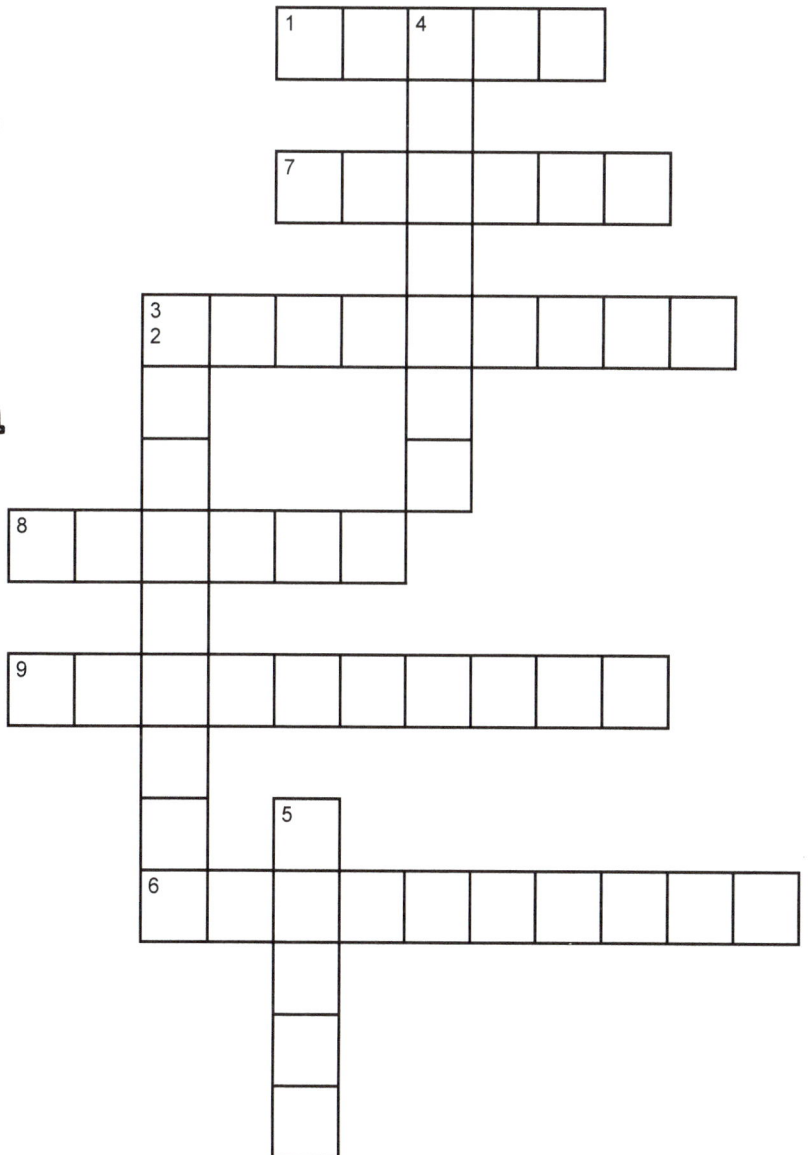

1.

2.

3.

4.

5.

6.

7.

8.

9.

Practice speaking Thai by playing the game!

Wat Phra Kâew Wat Àrun Tàlàat nát Jà-tù-jàk Săo Ching Cháa Yao-wá-ràat Bâahn

31	32	33 ?	34	35 ?	36 FINISH! You are home.
30 ?	29	28	27 ?	26	25 ?
19	20	21 ?	22	23 ?	24
18	17 ?	16	15	14 ?	13
7 ?	8	9	10 ?	11	12 ?
6	5 ?	4	3 ?	2	1 START

Instructions:
1. Play the game with one or two other players. The youngest player starts.
2. Roll the dice. If you land on a question mark, one of the other players must ask you: "**Kun bpai têe năi ká/kráp?**"
3. You must answer using the clues in the grids according to your position. For instance, if you land on number 17, you must answer: "**Chăn/Pŏm bpai têe Wat Arun doy reuua ka/kráp**".
4. The player who cannot answer the question must go back two spaces!
5. The winner of the game is the first player to reach the finish.

PS: Counting must be done in Thai!

D 🖊 Some of the sentences are jumbled! Tick the correct sentence.

Example:
A ☐ Jing jing pǒm nèuuay!   I am really tired!
B ☑ Pǒm nèuuay jing jing!   ผม เหนื่อย จริงๆ
C ☐ Nèuuay jing jing!

List 1:
A ☐ Rao yùu têe nǎi ká?
B ☐ Ká têe nǎi rao yùu?
C ☐ Têe nǎi yùu ká rao?
เรา อยู่ ที่ ไหน คะ

List 2:
A ☐ Sǎo Ching Cháa têe rót bpai doy taxi Kwang.
B ☐ Kwang bpai têe Sǎo Ching Cháa doy rót taxi.
C ☐ Taxi Sǎo Ching Cháa rót doy Kwang bpai têe.
กวาง ไป ที่ เสา ชิง ช้า โดย รถ แท็กซี่

List 3:
A ☐ Kráp têe nêe jòrt.
B ☐ Nêe kráp têe jòrt.
C ☐ Jòrt têe nêe kráp.
จอด ที่ นี่ ครับ

E 🧩 Match and link the Thai words with the English words.

Pǒm bpai têe Wat Àrun kráp.
ผม ไป ที่ วัด อรุณ ครับ   **1**

A Stop here.

Rao yùu têe Sǎo Ching Cháa.
เรา อยู่ ที่ เสา ชิง ช้า   **2**

B I go to the temple by boat.

Jòrt têe nêe.
จอด ที่ นี่   **3**

C I am tired.

Chǎn nèuuay ka.
ฉัน เหนื่อย ค่ะ   **4**

D We walk back home.

Rao derrn glàp bâahn.
เรา เดิน กลับ บ้าน   **5**

E We are at the Giant Swing.

Chǎn bpai têe wat doy reuua ka.
ฉัน ไป ที่ วัด โดย เรือ ค่ะ   **6**

F I go to the Temple of Dawn.

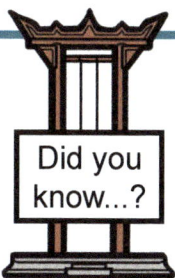

Giant Swing

Did you know...?

The Giant Swing (Sǎo Ching Cháa) was built in 1784 and is over 30 meters high! The swing Ceremony consisted of trying to grab a bag of golden coins placed on one of the pillars. It was discontinued in 1935 after several fatal accidents!

A 🖊 Complete the sentences by choosing a word from the boxes.

reuua เรือ	chêuu ชื่อ	pǒm ผม	yùu อยู่	doy โดย	kun yaay คุณ ยาย

1. Kawee bpai têe Wat Àrun doy _____.   กวี ไป ที่ วัด อรุณ โดย _____

2. Chăn _____ Phloi ka.   ฉัน _____ พลอย ค่ะ

3. Kwang gàp _____ yùu têe bâahn.   กวาง กับ _____ อยู่ ที่ บ้าน

4. _____ chêuu Tom kráp.   _____ ชื่อ ทอม ครับ

5. Kun pô _____ têe bâahn.   คุณ พ่อ _____ ที่ บ้าน

6. Chăn bpai têe Yao-wá-ràat _____   ฉัน ไป ที่ เยาวราช _____
   rót túk-túk.   รถ ตุ๊กตุ๊ก

B 🖊 👄 Translate the following text in Thai and say it out loud.

1. Hello. My name is... _____

2. What is your name? _____

3. My name is Kawee. _____

4. I am fine, thank you. _____

C 🎨 Draw a picture according to the description below.

1. Rót fai fáa รถ ไฟฟ้า	2. Kun yaay คุณ ยาย	3. Reuua เรือ	4. Rót yon รถ ยนต์
5. Pêe chaay พี่ชาย	6. Krêuang bin เครื่อง บิน	7. Derrn เดิน	8. Kun mâae คุณ แม่

D 🖊 Turn the following sentences into questions.

A Using "**Mái**", turn each sentence into a question requiring a simple yes or no answer.

Example: Kwang nèuuay ka.
กวาง เหนื่อย ค่ะ

Q: Kwang nèuuay **mái** ká?
กวาง เหนื่อย ไหม คะ

1. Sa-baai dee kráp.
สบาย ดี ครับ
Q: _____

2. Sànuk ka.
สนุก ค่ะ
Q: _____

3. Kawee glàp bâahn ka.
กวี กลับ บ้าน ค่ะ
Q: _____

4. Yàak lên dûay gan kráp.
อยาก เล่น ด้วย กัน ครับ
Q: _____

B Turn the following sentences into questions using "**Têe nǎi**" (where).

Example: Kun yaay yùu têe Wat Arun ka.
คุณ ยาย อยู่ ที่ วัด อรุณ ค่ะ

Q: Kun yaay yùu **têe nǎi** ká?
คุณ ยาย อยู่ ที่ ไหน คะ

1. Kun pô yùu têe nêe ka.
คุณ พ่อ อยู่ ที่ นี่ คะ
Q: _____

2. Kawee yùu têe bâahn ka.
กวี อยู่ ที่ บ้าน ค่ะ
Q: _____

3. Rao yùu têe wat ka.
เรา อยู่ ที่ วัด ค่ะ
Q: _____

4. Kwang jà bpai têe talàat kráp.
กวาง จะ ไป ที่ ตลาด ครับ
Q: _____

C Turn the following sentences into questions using "**Krai**" (who).

Example: Nêe keuu kun dtaa ka.
นี่ คือ คุณ ตา ค่ะ

Q: Nêe keuu **krai** ká?
นี่ คือ ใคร คะ

1. Nân keuu kun mâae ka.
นั่น คือ คุณ แม่ คะ
Q: _____

2. Nân keuu kun yaay ka.
นั่น คือ คุณ ยาย คะ
Q: _____

3. Nêe keuu nóng sǎao kráp.
นี่ คือ น้องสาว ครับ
Q: _____

4. Nêe keuu kun pô kráp.
นี่ คือ คุณ พ่อ ครับ
Q: _____

E ✏️ **Create sentences using the following words:**

Example: Reuua เรือ - Chǎn bpai têe Wat Arun doy **reuua** ka. ฉัน ไป ที่ วัด อรุณ โดย เรือ ค่ะ

1. Kun mâae   คุณ แม่ _____
2. A-rai   อะไร _____
3. Chêuu   ชื่อ _____
4. Bpai   ไป _____
5. Têe   ที่ _____
6. Rót meh   รถ เมล์ _____
7. Têe nǎi   ที่ ไหน _____
8. Rao   เรา _____
9. Chǎn   ฉัน _____
10. Wat   วัด _____

F 🧩 **Match and link the Thai words with the English words.**

Chǎn chêuu Kwang ka.
ฉัน ชื่อ กวาง ค่ะ   **1**

Sà-wàtdee kráp
สวัสดี ครับ   **2**

Nêe keuu pêe chaay ka.
นี่ คือ พี่ชาย ค่ะ   **3**

Chǎn yùu têe bâahn ka.
ฉัน อยู่ ที่ บ้าน ค่ะ   **4**

Sa-baai dee mái kráp?
สบาย ดี ไหม ครับ   **5**

Rao bpai têe wat ka.
เรา ไป ที่ วัด ค่ะ   **6**

Kun chêuu a-rai ká?
คุณ ชื่อ อะไร คะ   **7**

Chǎn glàp bâahn doy rót
meh ka.   **8**
ฉัน กลับ บ้าน โดย รถ เมล์ ค่ะ

Nân keuu kun pô ka.
นั่น คือ คุณ พ่อ ค่ะ   **9**

Korpkun kráp.
ขอบคุณ ครับ   **10**

A How are you?

B That is my father.

C We go to the temple.

D This is my older brother.

E I go home by bus.

F My name is Kwang.

G Thank you.

H Hello.

I What's your name?

J I am at home.

Lesson 4 - Counting at the Beach
Bòttêe 4 - Náp lêhk têe chaai hàat
บทที่ ๔ – นับ เลข ที่ ชาย หาด

In this lesson, the student will learn the following:

- Numbers
- Plurals
- To look
- To have
- How many
- Classifiers

Tom, Kawee and Kwang are spending their holidays on the island of Ko Sămui.

1

Wannée rao jà tham a-rai dee kráp?

Bpai náp mà-práaw gan tè kráp.

Bpai ka!

2

Mà-práaw nèung luuk ka!

Mà-práaw sŏrng luuk kráp.

Mà-práaw săm luuk kráp.

3

Mà-práaw sèe luuk kráp.

Duu nôhn sì, ling bon tôn mà-práaw ka!

Mà-práaw hâa luuk gàp mà-práaw hòk luuk kráp.

4

Mà-práaw jèt luuk kráp.

Mà-práaw bpaaet luuk ka!

5

Mà-práaw gâo luuk kráp!

Mà-práaw sìp luuk kráp!

6

Rao mee mà-práaw gèe luuk kráp?

Nèung, sŏrng, săm, sèe, hâa, hòk, jèt, bpaaet, gâo, sìp!

Rao mee mà-práaw sìp luuk kráp.

Story Translation
Bòd plaae • บท แปล

1

Tom: Wannée rao jà tham a-rai dee kráp?
วันนี้ เรา จะ ทำ อะไร ดี ครับ

What will we do today?

Kawee: Bpai náp mà-práaw gan tè kráp.
ไป นับ มะพร้าว กัน เถอะ ครับ

Let's go count coconuts.

Kwang: Bpai ka!
ไป ค่ะ

Yes!

2

Kwang: Mà-práaw **nèung** luuk ka!
มะพร้าว หนึ่ง ลูก ค่ะ

One coconut!

Tom: Mà-práaw **sǒrng** luuk kráp.
มะพร้าว สอง ลูก ครับ

Two coconuts.

Kawee: Mà-práaw **sǎm** luuk kráp.
มะพร้าว สาม ลูก ครับ

Three coconuts.

3

Kwang: Duu nôhn sì, ling bon tôn mà-práaw ka!
ดู โน่น ซิ, ลิงบน ต้น มะพร้าว ค่ะ

Look over there, a monkey on the coconut tree!

Tom: Mà-práaw **sèe** luuk kráp.
มะพร้าว สี่ ลูก ครับ

Four coconuts.

Kawee: Mà-práaw **hâa** luuk gàp mà-práaw **hòk** luuk kráp.
มะพร้าว ห้า ลูก กับ มะพร้าว หก ลูก ครับ

Five and **six** coconuts.

4

Kawee: Mà-práaw **jèt** luuk kráp.
มะพร้าว เจ็ด ลูก ครับ

Seven coconuts.

Kwang: Mà-práaw **bpaaet** luuk ka!
มะพร้าว แปด ลูก ค่ะ

Eight coconuts!

5

Kawee: Mà-práaw **gâo** luuk kráp!
มะพร้าว เก้า ลูก ครับ

Nine coconuts!

Tom: Mà-práaw **sìp** luuk kráp!
มะพร้าว สิบ ลูก ครับ

Ten coconuts!

6

Kawee: Rao mee mà-práaw gèe luuk kráp?
เรา มี มะพร้าว กี่ ลูก ครับ

How many coconuts do we have?

Kawee, Kwang and Tom: **Nèung, sǒrng, sǎm, sèe, hâa, hòk, jèt, bpaaet, gâo, sìp!**
หนึ่ง สอง สาม สี่ ห้า หก เจ็ด แปด เก้า สิบ

One, two, three, four, five, six, seven, eight, nine, ten!

Tom: Rao mee mà-práaw **sìp** luuk kráp.
เรา มี มะพร้าว สิบ ลูก ครับ

We have **ten** coconuts.

Vocabulary
Kamsàp • คำศัพท์

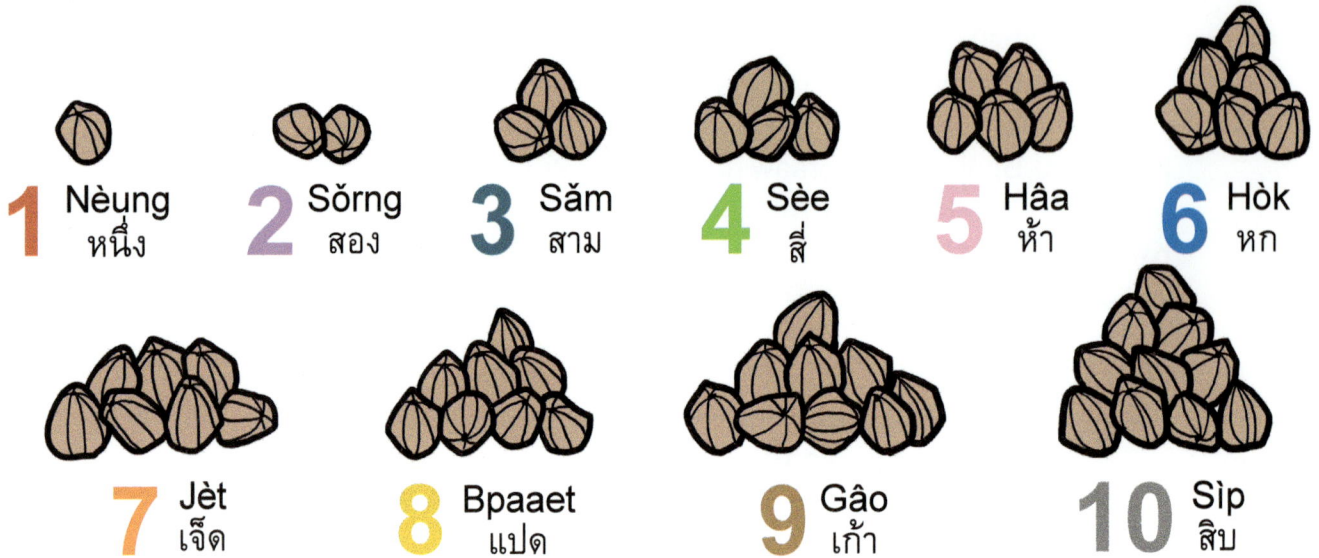

1 Nèung หนึ่ง
2 Sŏrng สอง
3 Săm สาม
4 Sèe สี่
5 Hâa ห้า
6 Hòk หก

7 Jèt เจ็ด
8 Bpaaet แปด
9 Gâo เก้า
10 Sìp สิบ

11	sìp et	สิบเอ็ด
12	sìp sŏrng	สิบสอง
13	sìp săm	สิบสาม
14	sìp sèe	สิบสี่
15	sìp hâa	สิบห้า
16	sìp hòk	สิบหก
17	sìp jèt	สิบเจ็ด
18	sìp bpaaet	สิบแปด
19	sìp gâo	สิบเก้า
20	yee sìp	ยี่สิบ

Find a complete list of numbers on page 80.

Lêhk	เลข	Number
Chaai hàat	ชาย หาด	Beach
Tham	ทำ	To do
Náp	นับ	To count
Mà-práaw	มะพร้าว	Coconut
Tôn mà-práaw	ต้น มะพร้าว	Coconut tree
Duu	ดู	To look
Ling	ลิง	Monkey
Bon	บน	On
Mee	มี	To have
Gèe	กี่	How many

Grammar and language notes
Waiya gawn gàp paa-săa • ไวยากรณ์ กับ ภาษา

classifiers Classifiers are words used in sentences to accompany a noun.

Khòn is the classifier used for people.
   e.g. Dèk **khòn** nân   That child
Tuua is the classifier used for animals.
   e.g. Plaa **tuua** nêe   This fish
Luuk is the classifier used for round fruits.
   e.g. Mà-práaw nèung **luuk** One coconut

gèe The word "**gèe**" means "**how many**".

Rao mee mà-práaw **gèe** luuk?
How many coconuts do we have?

mee The verb "**to have**" can be expressed by "**mee**".

Chăn **mee** năng-sĕuu nèung lèm.
I **have** one book.

Rao **mee** mà-práaw jèt luuk.
We **have** seven coconuts.

plural form Common nouns do not vary to indicate the plural form.

Mà-práaw nèung luuk   One coconut
Mà-práaw sŏrng luuk   Two coconuts

See Grammar and Language Notes for more details on **gèe** (p. 73), the verb **mee** (p.76), the **classifiers** (p.79) and the **plural form** (p.79).

Exercises
Baaep-fèuk-hàt • แบบ ฝึก หัด

A

Link the word to the corresponding number on the coconut.

Săm
สาม **A**

Hâa
ห้า **B**

Sìp
สิบ **C**

Gâo
เก้า **D**

Jèt
เจ็ด **E**

F Hòk
หก

G Sèe
สี่

H Bpaaet
แปด

I Sŏrng
สอง

J Nèung
หนึ่ง

B

Draw the number of items as requested.

Example: Mà-práaw săm luuk   Draw
มะพร้าว สาม ลูก   **3 coconuts**

1. Dèk hâa khòn   เด็ก ห้า คน

2. Ling bpaaet tuua   ลิง แปด ตัว

3. Tôn mà-práaw hòk tôn*   ต้น มะพร้าว หก ต้น

4. Mà-práaw sèe luuk   มะพร้าว สี่ ลูก

* **Tôn** is the classifier for trees.

C 🧩 Match and link the Thai words with the English words.

Mà-práaw sèe luuk
มะพร้าว สี่ ลูก **1**

Náp mà-práaw gan tè.
นับ มะพร้าว กัน เถอะ **2**

Ling jèt tuua
ลิง เจ็ด ตัว **3**

Rao mee mà-práaw gâo luuk.
เรา มี มะพร้าว เก้า ลูก **4**

Ling bon tôn mà-práaw
ลิง บน ต้น มะพร้าว **5**

Kun mee ling gèe tuua ká?
คุณ มี ลิง กี่ ตัว คะ **6**

A A monkey on a coconut tree.

B We have nine coconuts.

C Seven monkeys

D How many monkeys do you have?

E Let's count coconuts.

F Four coconuts

D 🧩 Tick the "number" in each line.

Example: ☐ chêuu ☐ yài ☐ mâae ✓ nèung ☐ lên

1. ☐ plaa • ปลา ☐ ling • ลิง ☐ sǒrng • สอง ☐ bon • บน ☐ mà-práaw • มะพร้าว
2. ☐ luuk • ลูก ☐ gèe • กี่ ☐ muàng • ม่วง ☐ sìp • สิบ ☐ mâae • แม่
3. ☐ dtào • เต่า ☐ dam • ดำ ☐ yùu • อยู่ ☐ pǒm • ผม ☐ hâa • ห้า
4. ☐ châwp • ชอบ ☐ ka • ค่ะ ☐ duu • ดู ☐ sǎm • สาม ☐ láaew-gǒr • แล้วก็
5. ☐ chǎn • ฉัน ☐ gâo • เก้า ☐ kráp • ครับ ☐ chêuu • ชื่อ ☐ korpkun • ขอบคุณ
6. ☐ sànuk • สนุก ☐ krai • ใคร ☐ nân • นั่น ☐ dtaa • ตา ☐ jèt • เจ็ด

E ✏️ Translate into Thai.

1. Eight coconuts. _____

2. What will we do today? _____

3. Go _____

4. How many monkeys do we have? _____

5. Ten monkeys _____

6. We have five coconuts. _____

Did you know...?

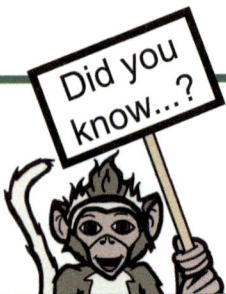

Trained monkeys

There are over 3,000,000 coconut trees on the island of Sǎmui! Trained monkeys climb the trees to pick only the ripe coconuts and drop them to the ground! Every month, an average of 2,000,000 coconuts are transported to Bangkok for consumption.

Lesson 5 - Colours at the Aquarium
Bòttêe 5 - Sĕe têe pipíttapan sàtnám
บทที่ ๕ – สี ที่ พิพิธภัณฑ์ สัตว์น้ำ

In this lesson, the student will learn the following:

- Colours
- To like
- Future tense

Story - Colours at the Aquarium
Sĕe têe pipíttapan sàtnám • สี ที่ พิพิธภัณฑ์ สัตวน้ำ

It is the weekend. Kawee and his friend Kataleeya are spending the afternoon at the aquarium with his parents.

1. Wannée rao jà bpai têe pipíttapan sàtnám ka.

Kataleeya maa gàp rao dâi mái kráp?

Dâi ka.

2. Duu plaa sĕe chompuu ka!

Tuua née sĕe daaeng gàp sĕe mûuang kráp.

3. Pŏm châwp tuua sĕe fáa gàp sĕe lĕuuang kráp. Luuk, châwp sĕe a-rai kráp?

Pŏm châwp tuua sĕe dam, sĕe sôm gàp sĕe kăaw kráp.

4. Duu nán si, dtào sĕe kĕeo ka!

Pŏm châwp dtào kráp!

5. Rao gamlang yùu tâi plaa chà-lăm sĕe tao kráp.

Chăn châwp plaa sĕe nám taan mâak gwàa ka.

6. Kun châwp sĕe a-rai têe sùt ká?

Chăn châwp sĕe mûuang gàp sĕe daaeng ka.

Pŏm châwp sĕe sôm kráp!

1 Kawee's mum: Wanneé rao jà bpai têe pipíttapan sàtnám ka.
วันนี้ เรา จะ ไป ที่ พิพิธภัณฑ์ สัตว์น้ำ ค่ะ

Today, we will go to the aquarium.

Kawee: Kataleeya maa gàp rao dâi mái kráp?
แคทลียา มา กับ เรา ได้ ไหม ครับ

Can Kataleeya come with us?

Kawee's mum: Dâi ka.
ได้ ค่ะ

Yes, she can.

2 Kataleeya: Duu plaa **sěe chompuu** ka!
ดู ปลา สี ชมพู ค่ะ

Look at the **pink** fish!

Kawee: Tuua née **sěe daaeng** gàp **sěe mûuang** kráp.
ตัว นี้ สี แดง กับ สี ม่วง ครับ

This one is **red** and **purple**.

3 Kawee's dad: Pǒm châwp tuua **sěe fáa** gàp **sěe lěuuang** kráp.
ผม ชอบ ตัว สี ฟ้า กับ สี เหลือง ครับ

I like the **blue** and **yellow** one.

Luuk, châwp sěe a-rai kráp?
ลูก ชอบ สี อะไร ครับ

Son, which colour do you like?

Kawee: Pǒm châwp tuua **sěe dam**, **sěe sôm** gàp **sěe kǎaw** kráp.
ผม ชอบ ตัว สี ดำ สี ส้ม กับ สี ขาว ครับ

I like the **black**, **orange** and **white** one.

4 Kataleeya: Duu nán si, dtào **sěe kěeo** ka!
ดู นั่น ซิ เต่า สี เขียว ค่ะ

Look at that one, the **green** turtle!

Kawee: Pǒm châwp dtào kráp!
ผม ชอบ เต่า ครับ

I like turtles!

5 Kawee: Rao gamlang yùu tâi plaa chà-lǎm **sěe tao** kráp.
เรา กำลัง อยู่ ใต้ ปลา ฉลาม สี เทา ครับ

We are under the **grey** sharks!

Kataleeya: Chǎn châwp plaa **sěe nám taan** mâak gwàa ka.
ฉัน ชอบ ปลา สี น้ำตาล มาก กว่า ค่ะ

I prefer the **brown** fish.

6 Kawee's mum: Kun châwp sěe a-rai têe sùt ká?
คุณ ชอบ สี อะไร ที่ สุด คะ

Which colour do you like most?

Kataleeya: Chǎn châwp **sěe mûuang** gàp **sěe daaeng** ka.
ฉัน ชอบ สี ม่วง กับ สี แดง ค่ะ

I like **purple** and **red**.

Kawee: Pǒm châwp **sěe sôm** kráp!
ผม ชอบ สี ส้ม ครับ

I like **orange**!

Vocabulary
Kamsàp • คำศัพท์

Sěe daaeng
สี แดง
Red

Sěe mûuang
สี ม่วง
Purple

Sěe nám ngen
สี น้ำ เงิน
Dark Blue

Sěe kěeo
สี เขียว
Green

Sěe fáa
สี ฟ้า
Light blue

Sěe chompuu
สี ชมพู
Pink

Sěe sôm
สี ส้ม
Orange

Sěe lěuuang
สี เหลือง
Yellow

Sěe nám taan
สี น้ำตาล
Brown

Sěe kǎaw
สี ขาว
White

Sěe tao
สี เทา
Grey

Sěe dam
สี ดำ
Black

Plaa	ปลา	Fish	Maa	มา	To come
Dtào	เต่า	Turtle	Châwp	ชอบ	To like
Plaa chà-lǎm	ปลา ฉลาม	Shark	Châwp mâak gwàa	ชอบมากกว่า	To prefer**
Luuk	ลูก	Son or daughter	Tuua	ตัว	Classifier*
Tâi	ใต้	Under	Gamlang	กำลัง	-ing ending**
Mâak	มาก	Very	Pipíttapan sàtnám	พิพิธภัณฑ์ สัตว์น้ำ	Aquarium
Têe sùt	ที่ สุด	The most			

* classifier for animals   ** See Grammar and Language Notes for more details on the verb to **prefer** (p.77) and **gamlang** (p.78).

Grammar and language notes
Waiya gawn gàp paa-sǎa • ไวยากรณ์ กับ ภาษา

sěe The word "**sěe**" is always displayed before the name of a colour. Without it, you might be saying someone's name!

Sěe dam   Black
Kun dam   Dam (someone's first name)

to be There is no verb "**to be**" used in front of adjectives and adverbs.

Plaa sěe fáa.   The fish is blue.
Tuua née sěe daaeng. This one is red.

jà One way of expressing the future tense is to place the word "**jà**" in front of the verb.

Chǎn **jà** pûut paa-sǎa Thai.
I will speak Thai.

Pǒm **jà** bpai têe wat.
I will go to the temple.

Kǎo **jà** lên footbawl.
He will play football.

See Grammar and Language Notes for more details on the verb **to be** (p.76) and the **future tense jà** (p.78).

Exercises
Baaep-fèuk-hàt • แบบ ฝึก หัด

 **A** Which colour is it?

1. **Sěe d** _ _ _ _ **g**   สี แดง
2. **Sěe c** _ _ _ **p** _ _   สี ชมพู
3. **Sěe f** _ _   สี ฟ้า
4. **Sěe n** _ _ **t** _ _ _   สี น้ำตาล
5. **Sěe t** _ _   สี เทา

6. **Sěe d** _ _   สี ดำ
7. **Sěe l** _ _ _ _ _ _   สี เหลือง
8. **Sěe m** _ _ _ _ _   สี ม่วง
9. **Sěe k** _ _ _   สี เขียว

 **B** Some of the sentences are jumbled! Tick the correct sentence.

List 1:
A ☐ Châwp pŏm plaa kráp chà-lăm.
B ☐ Pŏm châwp plaa chà-lăm kráp.
C ☐ Pŏm kráp chà-lăm plaa châwp.
ผม ชอบ ปลา ฉลาม ครับ

List 2:
A ☐ Chăn sěe daaeng mâak gwàa châwp ka.
B ☐ Chăn mâak châwp daaeng ka sěe gwàa.
C ☐ Chăn châwp sěe daaeng mâak gwàa ka.
ฉัน ชอบ สี แดง มาก กว่า ค่ะ

List 3:
A ☐ Duu plaa sěe fáa ka!
B ☐ Plaa duu fáa sěe ka!
C ☐ Ka sěe duu plaa fáa!
ดู ปลา สี ฟ้า ค่ะ

List 4:
A ☐ Kěeo châwp sěe Kawee.
B ☐ Kawee châwp sěe kěeo.
C ☐ Kěeo sěe châwp Kawee.
กวี ชอบ สี เขียว

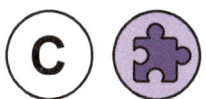 **C** Match and link the Thai words with the English words.

Plaa sěe nám taan
ปลา สี น้ำตาล **1**

Dtào sěe kěeo
เต่า สี เขียว **2**

Chăn châwp sěe chompuu ka.
ฉัน ชอบ สี ชมพู ค่ะ **3**

Pipíttapan sàtnám
พิพิธภัณฑ์ สัตว์น้ำ **4**

Pŏm châwp dtào kráp.
ผม ชอบ เต่า ครับ **5**

Pŏm châwp sěe daaeng kráp.
ผม ชอบ สี แดง ครับ **6**

A I like pink.

B Aquarium

C Brown fish

D I like turtles.

E I like red.

F Green turtle

1. Sĕe lĕuuang   สี เหลือง
2. Sĕe fáa   สี ฟ้า
3. Sĕe chompuu   สี ชมพู
4. Sĕe kăaw   สี ขาว
5. Sĕe mûuang   สี ม่วง
6. Sĕe sôm   สี ส้ม
7. Sĕe nám taan   สี น้ำตาล
8. Sĕe dam   สี ดำ
9. Sĕe kĕeo   สี เขียว
10. Sĕe daaeng   สี แดง
11. Sĕe tao   สี เทา
12. Sĕe nám ngen   สี น้ำเงิน

E ✏️   Translate into Thai.

1. The orange and white fish _____

2. I like black and yellow. _____

3. The green turtle _____

4. The grey shark _____

5. We will go to the aquarium. _____

6. I prefer red. _____

Did you know...?

Days of the Week

Monday	Tuesday	Wednesday	Thursday	Friday	Saturday	Sunday
Sĕe lĕuuang	Sĕe chompuu	Sĕe kĕeo	Sĕe sôm	Sĕe fáa	Sĕe mûuang	Sĕe daaeng

In Thai tradition, each day of the week is assigned a colour. These colours are also the traditional Thai Birthday colours. For example, if you are born on a Wednesday, your birth colour is green (sĕe kĕeo). Some Thai people dress according to the traditional colours. For instance, on Thursday, they wear orange clothes. What day is it today and what would you wear according to the Thai Birthday colours?

Lesson 6 - In the Classroom
Bòttêe 6 - Năi hôrng reean
บทที่ ๖ – ใน ห้อง เรียน

In this lesson, the student will learn the following:

- Objects in the classroom
- Question sentence using "châi mái"
- What
- The preposition "and" using "láaew-gôr" or "gàp"

The students are having their Thai lesson at their international school.

1
Sà-wàtdee ka nák-reean. Nâng long ka.

Nák-reean, kao-rób!

Sà-wàtdee ka kun kruu.

Sà-wàtdee kráp kun kruu.

2
Wannée, rao jà pûut paa-săa Thai năi hôrng reean nà ká.

Yìp sa-mùd gàp din-sŏr nà ká.

3
Nêe keuu a-rai kráp? Nêe keuu sa-mùd châi mái kráp?

Mâi châi kráp. Nân keuu năng-sĕuu kráp.

Nêe keuu sa-mùd kráp.

4
Nák reean, yìp gra-dàat, láaew-gôr gan-grai, láaew-gôr gaao, láaew-gôr din-sŏr sĕe gàp mái-ban-tát nà ká.

5
Reean paa-săa Thai sànuk ka!

Châi ká!

6
Gèng mâak ka.

Story Translation
Bòd plaae • บท แปล

1

Kawee: Nák-reean, kao-rób!
นักเรียน เคารพ

Students, pay respect!

Students: Sà-wàtdee ka/kráp kun kruu.
สวัสดี ค่ะ/ครับ คุณ ครู

Good morning teacher.

Kun kruu: Sà-wàtdee ka nák-reean.
สวัสดี ค่ะ นักเรียน

Good morning students.

Nâng long ka.
นั่ง ลง ค่ะ

Sit down please.

2

Kun kruu: Wannée, rao jà pûut paa-săa Thai năi hôrng reean nà ká.
วันนี้ เรา จะ พูด ภาษา ไทย ใน ห้อง เรียน นะ คะ

Today we will speak Thai in the classroom.

Yìp **sa-mùd** gàp **din-sŏr** nà ká.
หยิบ สมุด กับ ดินสอ นะ คะ

Take your **notebook** and your **pencil** please.

3

Tom: Nêe keuu a-rai kráp?
นี่ คือ อะไร ครับ?

What is this?

Nêe keuu **sa-mùd** châi mái kráp?
นี่ คือ สมุด ใช่ ไหม ครับ?

Is this a **notebook**?

Kawee: Mâi châi kráp.
ไม่ ใช่ ครับ

No.

Nân keuu **năng-sĕuu** kráp.
นั่น คือ หนังสือ ครับ

That is a **book**.

Nêe keuu **sa-mùd** kráp.
นี่ คือ สมุด ครับ

This is a **notebook**.

4

Kun kruu: Nák reean, yìp **gra-dàat**, láaew-gôr **gan-grai**, láaew-gôr **gaao**, láaew-gôr **din-sŏr sĕe** gàp **mái-ban-tát** nà ká.
นัก เรียน หยิบ กระดาษ แล้วก็ กรรไกร แล้วก็ กาว แล้วก็ ดินสอ สี กับ ไม้บรรทัด นะ คะ

Students, take some **paper**, **scissors**, **glue**, **crayons** and a **ruler** please.

5

Phloi: Reean paa-săa Thai sànuk ka!
เรียน ภาษา ไทย สนุก ค่ะ

Learning Thai is fun!

Kataleeya: Châi ka!
ใช่ ค่ะ

Yes, it is.

6

Kun kruu: Gèng mâak ka.
เก่ง มาก ค่ะ

Well done.

Vocabulary
Kamsàp • คำศัพท์

Sa-mùd
สมุด
Notebook

Din-sŏr
ดินสอ
Pencil

Năng-sĕuu
หนังสือ
Book

Kun kruu
คุณ ครู
Teacher

Nák-reean
นักเรียน
Student

Gra-dàat
กระดาษ
Paper

Gan-grai
กรรไกร
Scissors

Gaao
กาว
Glue

Kao-rób	เคารพ	Pay respect
Nâng long	นั่ง ลง	Sit down
Wannée	วันนี้	Today
Pûut	พูด	Speak
Paa-săa	ภาษา	Language
Thai	ไทย	Thai
Năi	ใน	In
Hôrng reean	ห้อง เรียน	Classroom
Yìp	หยิบ	Take
Láaew-gôr	แล้วก็	And
Nà	นะ	Polite article
Reean	เรียน	To study
Gèng mâak	เก่ง มาก	Well done
Châi /Mâi châi	ใช่/ไม่ ใช่	Yes/No

Din-sŏr sĕe
ดินสอ สี
Crayons

Mái-ban-tát
ไม้บรรทัด
Ruler

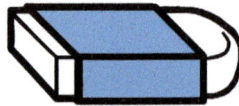

Yaang-lóp
ยางลบ
Eraser

Grammar and language notes
Waiya gawn gàp paa-săa • ไวยากรณ์ กับ ภาษา

(a-rai) The word "**a-rai**" means "**what**".

Nêe keuu **a-rai**?　　**What** is this?
Nân keuu **a-rai**?　　**What** is that?

(châi mái) "**Châi mái**" can be used when seeking confirmation to the assumption made in the question. The answer is formed using "**châi**" for "**yes**" and "**mâi châi**" for "**no**".

Nêe keuu sa-mùd **châi mái**?
This is a notebook, isn't it?

Mâi châi.　**No**, it is not.
Châi.　　**Yes**, it is.

(láaew-gôr & gàp) In Thai, when enumerating more than 2 items in a sentence, "**láaew-gôr**" is used to say "**and**".

However, for enumerating only 2 items, "**gàp**" can be used.

(definite or indefinite article) In Thai, there is no definite or indefinite article placed in front of a noun.

Nêe keuu năng-sĕuu.　This is **(a)** book.
Chăn yìp sa-mùd.　　I take **(the)** notebook.

See Grammar and Language Notes for more details on the word **and** (p.74), the use of **châi mái** (p.73) and **a-rai** (p.74).

Exercises
Baaep-fèuk-hàt • แบบ ฝึก หัด

A 🧩 Match and link the Thai words with the English words.

Nêe keuu sa-mùd. **1**
นี่ คือ สมุด

A This is not a book.

Nák-reean **2**
นัก เรียน

B To study

Gèng mâak. **3**
เก่ง มาก

C This is a notebook.

Nêe mâi châi năng-sĕuu. **4**
นี่ ไม่ ใช่ หนังสือ

D Well done.

Kun kruu **5**
คุณ ครู

E Student

Reean **6**
เรียน

F Teacher

B 🧩 Tick the "classroom object" in each list.

Example: ☐ chêuu ☐ kráp ☐ mâae ☑ gaao ☐ lên

List 1:
☐ A-rai • อะไร
☐ Chăn • ฉัน
☐ Ka • ค่ะ
☐ Plaa • ปลา
☐ Sa-mùd • สมุด

List 2:
☐ Dèk • เด็ก
☐ Korpkun • ขอบคุณ
☐ Mûang • ม่วง
☐ Gan-grai • กรรไกร
☐ Mâae • แม่

List 3:
☐ Nêe • นี่
☐ Rao • เรา
☐ Gra-dàat • กระดาษ
☐ Pûut • พูด
☐ Sànuk • สนุก

List 4:
☐ Yàak • อยาก
☐ Năng-sĕuu • หนังสือ
☐ Duu • ดู
☐ Săm • สาม
☐ Láaew-gôr • แล้วก็

List 5:
☐ Gàp • กับ
☐ Wannée • วันนี้
☐ Châi • ใช่
☐ Kun • คุณ
☐ Din-sŏr • ดินสอ

List 6:
☐ Mâak • มาก
☐ Krai • ใคร
☐ Yaang-lòp • ยางลบ
☐ Nák-reean • นักเรียน
☐ Kruu • ครู

C ✏️ Translate into Thai.

1. Sit down please. _____

2. Well done students! _____

3. Please take your ruler. _____

4. Is this a crayon? _____

5. This is a pencil. _____

6. That is a pencil. _____

D ✏️ Answer the questions related to each picture.

Example 1:
Q: Nêe keuu sa-mùd châi mái ká?
นี่ คือ สมุด ใช่ ไหม คะ?
Is this a notebook?
A: *Châi ka. Nêe keuu sa-mùd ka.*
ใช่ ค่ะ นี่ คือ สมุด ค่ะ
Yes. It is a notebook.

Example 2:
Q: Nêe keuu din-sŏr châi mái ká?
นี่ คือ ดินสอ ใช่ ไหม คะ?
Is this a pencil?
A: *Mâi châi ka. Nêe keuu yaang-lóp ka.*
ไม่ ใช่ ค่ะ นี่ คือ ยางลบ ค่ะ
No. It is an eraser.

1. Q: Nêe keuu gra-dàat châi mái ká/kráp?   นี่ คือ กระดาษ ใช่ ไหม คะ/ครับ?

   A: _____

2. Q: Nêe keuu năng-sĕuu châi mái ká/kráp?   นี่ คือ หนังสือ ใช่ ไหม คะ/ครับ?

   A: _____

3. Q: Nêe keuu gan-grai châi mái ká/kráp?   นี่ คือ กรรไกร ใช่ ไหม คะ/ครับ?

   A: _____

4. Q: Nêe keuu mái-ban-tát châi mái ká/kráp?   นี่ คือ ไม้บรรทัด ใช่ ไหม คะ/ครับ?

   A: _____

5. Q: Nêe keuu din-sŏr sĕe châi mái ká/kráp?   นี่ คือ ดินสอสี ใช่ ไหม คะ/ครับ?

   A: _____

6. Q: Nêe keuu din-sŏr châi mái ká/kráp?   นี่ คือ ดินสอ ใช่ ไหม คะ/ครับ?

   A: _____

Complete the crossword using the picture clues.

1.

2.

3.

4.

5.

6.

7.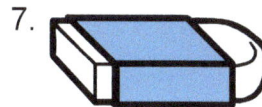

8.

9.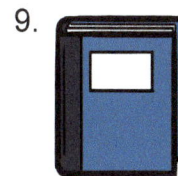

Meditation

In Thai schools, students are taught to meditate from an early age and often spend about 5-10 minutes a day for meditation. Even kindergarten children meditate and their teachers believe it helps them to calm down and to sleep better.

Did you know...?

Lessons 4 - 6 Revision Exercises

A ✏️ Complete the sentences by choosing a word from the boxes.

paa-săa ภาษา	nák-reean นักเรียน	sìp สิบ	sěe daaeng สี แดง	kěeo เขียว	hâa ห้า

1. Rao mee mà-práaw _____ luuk kráp. เรา มี มะพร้าว _____ ลูก ครับ

2. Pŏm châwp _____ kráp. ผม ชอบ _____ ครับ

3. Dtào sěe _____ ka. เต่า สี _____ ค่ะ

4. _____ yùu năi hôrng reean. _____ อยู่ ใน ห้อง เรียน

5. Reean _____ Thai sànuk mâak ka. เรียน _____ ไทย สนุก มาก ค่ะ

6. Nèung, sŏrng, săm, sèe, _____, hòk, jèt, bpaaet, gâo, sìp. หนึ่ง สอง สาม สี่ _____ หก เจ็ด แปด เก้า สิบ

B ✏️ Choose the correct classifier and translate.

Complete the sentences below, using the correct classifier from the following boxes then translate afterwards. Please make sure you study the rules about the **classifiers** (p.79) before doing this exercise.

khòn คน	tuua ตัว	luuk ลูก	lèm เล่ม	àn อัน

Example: Choose classifier: Ling sìp **tuua**. ลิง สิบ ตัว   Translate: Ten monkeys.

Choose classifier: Translate:

1. Plaa săm _____   ปลา สาม ____   _____

2. Năng-sěuu bpaaet _____   หนังสือ แปด ____   _____

3. Dèk sèe _____   เด็ก สี่ ____   _____

4. Mà-práaw hâa _____   มะพร้าว ห้า ____   _____

5. Dtào nèung _____   เต่า หนึ่ง ____   _____

6. Pêuuan jèt _____   เพื่อน เจ็ด ____   _____

7. Sa-mùd gâo _____   สมุด เก้า ____   _____

8. Gan-grai sŏrng _____   กรรไกร สอง ____   _____

9. Yaang-lóp hòk _____   ยางลบ หก ____   _____

10. Mái-ban-tát sìp _____   ไม้บรรทัด สิบ ____   _____

C ✏️ Answer the questions using the number as part of the answer.

Answer the following "Gèe?" (How many?) questions using the numbers in brackets. Don't forget the classifiers!

Example: Q: Mee mà-práaw gèe luuk ká? **(7)**   A: Jèt luuk ka.
มี มะพร้าว กี่ ลูก คะ   เจ็ด ลูก ค่ะ
How many coconuts are there?   Seven coconuts.

1. Q: Mee năng-sĕuu gèe lèm ká? **(8)**   A: _____
มี หนังสือ กี่ เล่ม คะ

2. Q: Mee pêuuan gèe khòn kráp? **(5)**   A: _____
มี เพื่อน กี่ คน ครับ

3. Q: Mee ling gèe tuua ká? **(3)**   A: _____
มี ลิง กี่ ตัว คะ

4. Q: Mee plaa gèe tuua ká? **(2)**   A: _____
มี ปลา กี่ ตัว คะ

5. Q: Mee dtào gèe tuua kráp? **(4)**   A: _____
มี เต่า กี่ ตัว ครับ

6. Q: Mee gan-grai gèe lèm ká? **(6)**   A: _____
มี กรรไกร กี่ เล่ม คะ

D ✏️ Create sentences using the following words:

1. Hòk   หก   _____

2. Châwp   ชอบ   _____

3. Sĕe fáa   สี ฟ้า   _____

4. Kun kruu   คุณ ครู   _____

5. Paa-săa thai ภาษา ไทย _____

6. Wannée   วันนี้   _____

7. Sĕe sôm   สี ส้ม   _____

8. Sìp   สิบ   _____

9. Hôrng reean ห้อง เรียน _____

10. Mee   มี   _____

1. Din-sǒr sěe
ดินสอ สี

2. Dtào sěe kěeo
เต่า สี เขียว

3. Plaa sěe daaeng
ปลา สี แดง

4. Ling sěe nám taan
ลิง สี น้ำ ตาล

5. Nǎng-sěuu
sěe dam
หนังสือ สี ดำ

6. Gan-grai
gàp gaao
กรรไกร กับ กาว

7. Mái-ban-tát
sěe chompuu
ไม้บรรทัด สี ชมพู

8. Mà-práaw
sǎm luuk
มะพร้าว สาม ลูก

F ✏️ Create a question and include the given word in an answer.

Write the question using "**Nêe keuu a-rai ká/kráp?**" for each item below, and answer accordingly.

Example:
Q: Nêe keuu a-rai ká?   นี่ คือ อะไร คะ   What is this?
A: **(Scissors)** Nêe keuu gan-grai ka.   นี่ คือ กรรไกร ค่ะ   These are scissors.

1. Q: _____
   A: (Paper) _____

2. Q: _____
   A: (Crayons) _____

3. Q: _____
   A: (Book) _____

4. Q: _____
   A: (Ruler) _____

5. Q: _____
   A: (Notebook) _____

6. Q: _____
   A: (Pencil) _____

Lesson 7 - At the Market
Bòttêe 7 - Têe tàlàat
บทที่ ๗ – ที่ ตลาด

In this lesson, the student will learn the following:

- Food names
- Food related adverbs
- To eat
- To drink
- Past tense
- To want

Story - At the Market
Têe tàlàat • ที่ ตลาด

The children are visiting a local food market with their teacher.

Story Translation
Bòd plaae • บท แปล

1   Kun kruu: Kǒr **ngau** ka.   I would like some **rambutans** please.
ขอ เงาะ ค่ะ

      Vendor: Aow gèe kilo ká?   How many kilos would you like?
เอา กี่ กิโล คะ

   Kun kruu: Nèung kilo ka.   One kilo please.
หนึ่ง กิโล ค่ะ

2   Phloi: Châwp gin **pàk** mái ká?   Do you like eating **vegetables**?
ชอบ กิน ผัก ไหม คะ

   Kataleeya: Châwp mâak ka.   Very much.
ชอบ มาก ค่ะ

3   Kawee: Pǒm hǐuw láaew kráp.   I am hungry.
ผม หิว แล้ว ครับ

      Vendor: Gin a-rai kráp?   What would you like to eat?
กิน อะไร ครับ

        Tom: Kǒr **gài** satay kráp.   I would like **chicken** satay please.
ขอ ไก่ สะเต๊ะ ครับ

4   Phloi :   Kǒr **kâao pad gài** ka.   I would like **chicken fried rice** please.
ขอ ข้าว ผัด ไก่ ค่ะ

     Kwang: Pèt mái ká?   Is it spicy?
เผ็ด ไหม คะ

      Phloi: Pèt nít nòy ka.   It is a little bit spicy.
เผ็ด นิด หน่อย ค่ะ

5   Kataleeya: Hǐuw nám mâak ka.   I am very thirsty.
หิว น้ำ มาก ค่ะ

                 Dèuum a-rai ká?   What are you drinking?
ดื่ม อะไร คะ

     Kwang: Dèuum nám **sàparót** ka.   I am drinking **pineapple juice**.
ดื่ม น้ำ สับปะรด ค่ะ

6   Tom: Gin **kanǒm** a-rai kráp?   What **dessert** are you eating?
กิน ขนม อะไร ครับ

     Kawee: Gin kâao nǐaw **ma-mûuang** kráp.   I am eating **mango** and sticky rice.
กิน ข้าว เหนียว มะม่วง ครับ

                 Aròy kráp!   It is delicious!
อร่อย ครับ

      Phloi: Hìm láaew ka!   I'm full!
อิ่ม แล้ว ค่ะ

Vocabulary
Kamsàp • คำศัพท์

Sàparót สับปะรด Pineapple	Sôm ส้ม Orange	Ma-mûuang มะม่วง Mango	Glûay กล้วย Banana	Malagor มะละกอ Papaya	Ngau เงาะ Rambutan	Kâao ข้าว Rice

Pàk ผัก Vegetables	Pǒnlamái ผลไม้ Fruits	Nám sôm น้ำ ส้ม Orange juice	Gài ไก่ Chicken	Gài satay ไก่ สะเต๊ะ Chicken satay	Kanǒm ขนม Dessert (or snack)

Kǒr	ขอ	…would like…	Kâao pad	ข้าว ผัด	Fried rice
Aow	เอา	Would you like?	Pèt	เผ็ด	Spicy
Gin	กิน	To eat	Aròy	อร่อย	Delicious
Dèuum	ดื่ม	To drink	Nám	น้ำ	Water
Hĭuw láaew	หิว แล้ว	To be hungry	Láaew	แล้ว	Past tense
Hìm láaew	อิ่ม แล้ว	To be full	Nít nòy	นิด หน่อย	A little bit
Hĭuw nám	หิว น้ำ	To be thirsty	Kilo	กิโล	Kilo

Grammar and language notes
Waiya gawn gàp paa-sǎa • ไวยากรณ์ กับ ภาษา

kǒr Asking for something in a restaurant, market, shop, etc… can be expressed using the verb "**kǒr**".

Chǎn **kǒr** ma-mûuang ka.
I would like some mango please.

Pǒm **kǒr** sàparót kráp.
I would like some pineapple please.

láaew The word "**láaew**" is often used to express an action that has already taken place. "**Láaew**" is also used for the following expressions:

Pǒm hǐuw **láaew** kráp. I am hungry(already).
Hìm **láaew** kráp.   I am full (already).

nám To name any fruit juice or other juice in Thai, you use the prefix nám (water).

Nám sàparót   Pineapple juice
Nám sôm   Orange juice

aow Asking someone if she/he wants something can be expressed using the verb "**aow**".

Aow nám sôm mái ká?
Would you like some orange juice?

Aow gài satay mái ká?
Would you like some chicken satay?

See Grammar and Language Notes for more details on the verbs kǒr and aow (p.77) and the use of láaew (p.78).

Exercises
Baaep-fèuk-hàt • แบบ ฝึก หัด

A 🧩 Match and link the Thai words with the English words.

Nám sàparót
น้ำ สับปะรด **1**

Kŏr nám sôm ka.
ขอ น้ำ ส้ม ค่ะ **2**

Pèt mâak.
เผ็ด มาก **3**

Pŏm hĭuw láaew kráp.
ผม หิว แล้ว ครับ **4**

Rao châwp kanŏm.
เรา ชอบ ขนม **5**

Nít nòy.
นิด หน่อย **6**

A I am hungry.

B We like desserts.

C A little bit.

D Pineapple juice

E It's very spicy.

F I would like orange juice please.

B ✏️ Translate into Thai.

1. Phloi is thirsty. _____

2. Kwang is hungry. _____

3. Tom is full. _____

4. What would you like to eat? _____

5. Delicious. _____

6. I like mango juice. _____

C 🧩 Find and circle the words in the grid.

1. Dèuum   ดื่ม
2. Pèt   เผ็ด
3. Aow   เอา
4. Nít nòy   นิด หน่อย
5. Kâao   ข้าว
6. Aròy   อร่อย
7. Pŏnlamái   ผลไม้
8. Kilo   กิโล
9. Gin   กิน
10. Kŏr   ขอ

A	B	W	U	G	I	N	B	P	A	T	H
D	E	U	U	M	X	K	X	E	R	Y	Q
R	N	H	F	R	K	J	L	T	P	X	J
P	O	N	L	A	M	A	I	J	V	L	C
B	Z	I	C	V	L	P	M	K	A	A	O
A	R	T	V	Q	K	X	T	D	P	O	S
R	L	N	D	T	G	B	H	I	E	W	L
O	N	O	S	K	O	R	N	R	G	E	T
Y	G	Y	E	O	F	H	X	K	I	L	O

D 🎨 | Draw in each box the food described below.

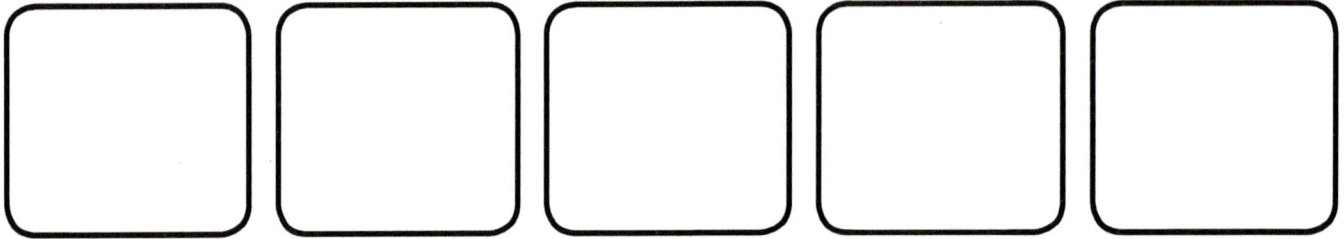

1.Sôm ส้ม	2. Sàparót สับปะรด	3. Kanŏm ขนม	4. Pàk ผัก	5. Gài ไก่

E 🎲 👄 | Practice speaking Thai by playing the game!

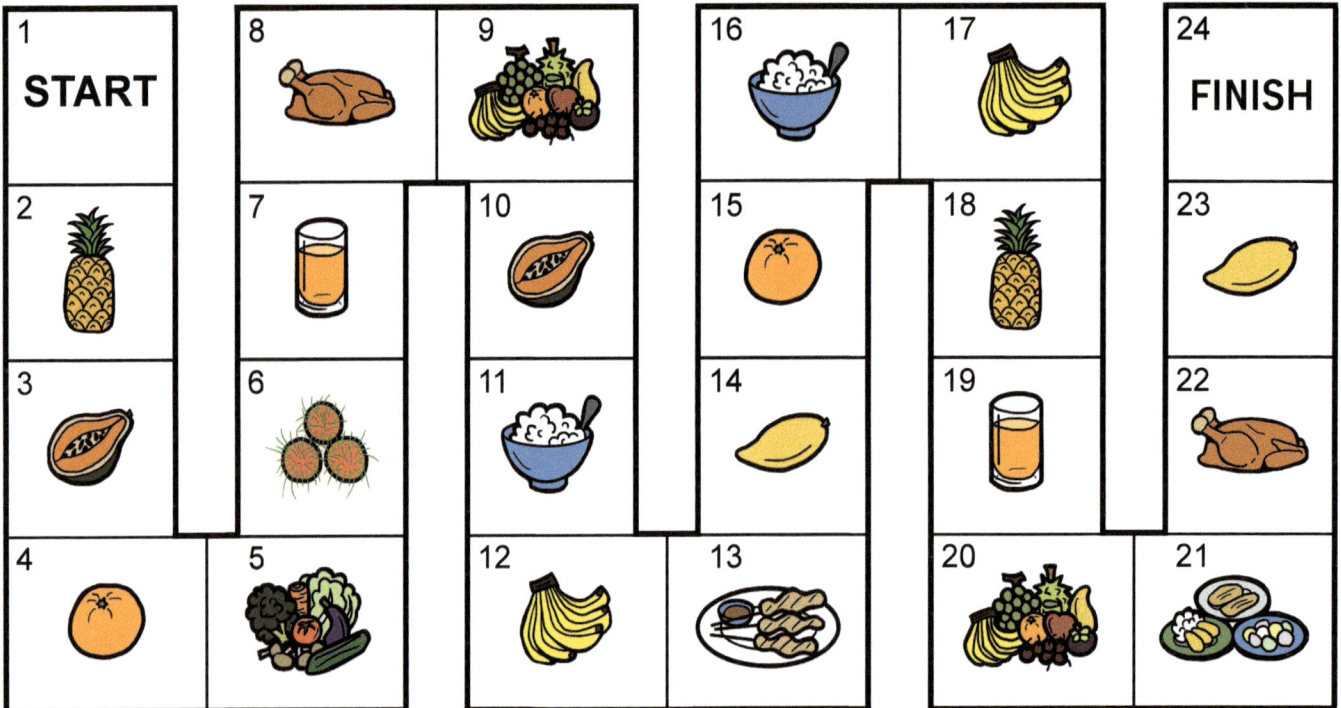

1 **START**	8	9		16	17	24 **FINISH**
2	7	10		15	18	23
3	6	11	14		19	22
4	5	12	13		20	21

Instructions:
1. Play the game with one or two other players. The youngest player starts.
2. Roll the dice. Another player must ask you "**Gin a-rai kráp/ká?**"
3. You must answer saying "**Pŏm/chăn kŏr (food symbol) kráp/ka.**"
4. For instance, if you land on a pineapple, you must answer "**Pŏm/chăn kŏr sàparót kráp/ka**".
5. The player who cannot answer the question must go back two spaces!
6. The winner of the game is the first player to reach the finish.
PS: Counting must be done in Thai!

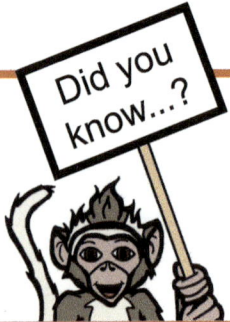

Did you know...?

Snacks

School children often buy food from street vendors right outside school. As an after school snack, they might buy BBQ pork and sticky rice, chicken balls or coconut ice-cream with sticky rice.

Lesson 8 - At the Zoo
Bòttêe 8 - Têe sǔan-sàt
บทที่ ๘ – ที่ สวน สัตว์

In this lesson, the student will learn the following:

- Animals
- To come
- Personal pronoun "it"
- Warning signs
- Adjectives

The children are visiting a zoo in Bangkok on a school trip.

Panel 1:
Kwang, maa duu yee-ráaf ka.
Man tuua sǔung mâak ka!
HÂAM HÂI AA-HǍAN!

Panel 2:
Sěuua-krôhng nâa-gluua kráp!
Yàa jàp ka!

Panel 3:
Cháang! Pǒm châwp cháang mâak kráp!
Man tuua yài láe kǎeng-raaeng ka!

Panel 4:
Maa duu pěe-sêuua kráp!
Man tuua lék láe sǔuay mâak ka!

Panel 5:
Duu nguu bon tônmái sì! Man mee-pít kráp!
Man tuua yaaw yaaw láe man léuuay reow ka.

Panel 6:
Jo-ra-kêh! Man klaan cháa cháa ka!
Yàa ta-gohn ka!
HÂAM KÂO!

Story Translation
Bòd plaae • บท แปล

1

Kataleeya: Kwang, maa duu **yee-ráaf** ka.
กวาง มา ดู ยีราฟ ค่ะ

Kwang, come look at the **giraffe**.

Kwang: Man tuua sǔung mâak ka!
มัน ตัว สูง มาก ค่ะ

It is very tall!

🚫 Hâam Hâi Aa-hǎan!   ห้าม ให้ อาหาร   No Feeding!

2

Kawee: **Sěuua-krôhng** nâa-gluua kráp!
เสือ โคร่ง น่า กลัว ครับ

The **tiger** is frightening!

Kun kruu: Yàa jàp ka!
อย่า จับ ค่ะ

Don't touch!

3

Kawee: **Cháang**!
ช้าง

Elephants!

Pǒm châwp cháang mâak kráp!
ผม ชอบ ช้าง มาก ครับ

I really like elephants!

Kwang: Man tuua yài láe kǎeng-raaeng ka!
มัน ตัว ใหญ่ และ แข็ง แรง ค่ะ

They are big and heavy!

4

Tom: Maa duu **pěe-sêuua** kráp!
มา ดู ผีเสื้อ ครับ

Come look at the **butterflies**!

Kataleeya: Man tuua lék láe sǔuay mâak ka!
มัน ตัว เล็ก และ สวย มาก ค่ะ

They are little and very pretty.

5

Kawee: Duu **nguu** bon tônmái sì!
ดู งู บน ต้นไม้ ซิ

Look at the **snake** in the tree!

Man mee-pít kráp!
มัน มี พิษ ครับ

It is poisonous!

Kataleeya: Man tuua yaaw yaaw láe man léuuay reow ka.
มัน ตัว ยาว ๆ และ มัน เลื้อย เร็ว ค่ะ

It is very long and it crawls rapidly.

6

Phloi: **Jo-ra-kêh**!
จระเข้

Crocodiles!

Man klaan cháa cháa ka!
มัน คลาน ช้า ๆ ค่ะ

They crawl so slowly!

Kun kruu: Yàa ta-gohn ka!
อย่า ตะโกน ค่ะ

Don't shout please!

🚫 Hâam Kâo!   ห้าม เข้า   No Entry!

Vocabulary
Kamsàp • คำศัพท์

Yee-ráaf
ยีราฟ
Giraffe

Sĕuua-krôhng
เสือ โคร่ง
Tiger

Cháang
ช้าง
Elephant

Pĕe-sêuua
ผีเสื้อ
Butterfly

Nguu
งู
Snake

Jo-ra-kêh
จระเข้
Crocodile

Kwaay
ควาย
Water Buffalo

Mǎa
หมา
Dog

Maaew
แมว
Cat

Sŭan-sàt	สวน สัตว์	Zoo	Léuuay	เลื้อย	To crawl*
Man	มัน	It	Cháa	ช้า	Slow
Láe	และ	And	Klaan	คลาน	To crawl**
Sŭung	สูง	Tall	Reow	เร็ว	Fast
Nâa gluua	น่า กลัว	Frightening	Ta-gohn	ตะโกน	To shout
Yài	ใหญ่	Big	Yàa	อย่า	Do not ….
Kăeng-raaeng	แข็ง แรง	Heavy	Jàp	จับ	To touch
Sŭuay	สวย	Pretty	Hâam	ห้าม	Forbidden to…
Lék	เล็ก	Small	Hâi aa-hǎan	ให้ อาหาร	To feed
Mee-pít	มี พิษ	Poisonous	Aa-hǎan	อาหาร	Food
Yaaw	ยาว	Long	Kâo	เข้า	Entry/to enter
Tônmái	ต้นไม้	Tree			

* animals with no legs (e.g. Snake) ** animals with four legs (e.g. Crocodile)

Grammar and language notes
Waiya gawn gàp paa-sǎa • ไวยากรณ์ กับ ภาษา

maa The verb "**to come**" can be expressed by "**maa**".

Maa nêe ka.	**Come** here.
Maa duu yee-ráaf ka.	**Come** see the giraffe.

láe "Láe" can be used to express the word "**and**" when using two expressions to describe one object/person/animal.

Cháang tuua yài **láe** kăeng-raaeng.
The elephant is big **and** heavy.

man The personal pronoun "**it**" can be expressed by "**man**".

Man tuua sŭung.	**It** is tall.
Man tuua yài.	**It** is big.

Note: In spoken Thai, one would say "Tuua man sŭung" instead of "Man tuua sŭung".

yàa & hâam Negative commands can be expressed by "**yàa**" or "**hâam**".

Yàa ta-gohn!	**Don't** shout!
Hâam hai aahaan.	**No** feeding. (Forbidden)

See Grammar and Language Notes for more details on the verb **maa** (p.77), the word **and** (p.74) and the verbs **yàa** and **hâam** (p.78).

Exercises
Baaep-fèuk-hàt • แบบ ฝึก หัด

A 🧩 Complete the crossword using the picture clues.

1.
2.
3.
4.
5.
6.
7.

B ✏️ Translate into Thai.

1. The giraffe is tall. _____

2. The butterfly is small. _____

3. The tiger is big. _____

4. The crocodile is frightening. _____

5. The elephant is big _____

6. The water buffalo is strong. _____

C 🎨 Draw in each box the animal described below.

1. Cháang tuua lék
   ช้าง ตัว เล็ก

2. Cháang tuua yài
   ช้าง ตัว ใหญ่

3. Pĕe-sêuua sŭuay
   ผีเสื้อ สวย

4. Pĕe-sêuua
   nâa-gluua!
   ผีเสื้อ น่า กลัว

hâam ห้าม	duu ดู	mee-pít มี พิษ	jo-ra-kêh จระเข้	sǔuay สวย	yàa อย่า

1. _____ klaan cháa cháa ka. จระเข้ คลาน ช้า ๆ ค่ะ

2. Pěe-sêuua _____ mâak ka. ผีเสื้อ สวย มาก ค่ะ

3. _____ hâi aa-hǎan! ห้าม ให้ อาหาร

4. Maa _____ yee-ráaf ka. มา ดู ยีราฟ ค่ะ

5. Nguu _____ ka. งู มี พิษ ค่ะ

6. _____ jap ka! อย่า จับ ค่ะ

Duu jo-ra-kêh sì.
ดู จระเข้ ซิ
1

A The elephant is very heavy.

Nguu yùu bon tônmái sì.
งู อยู่ บน ต้นไม้ ซิ
2

B It is tall.

Cháang kǎeng-raaeng mâak.
ช้าง แข็ง แรง มาก
3

C Don't go there.

Man tuua sǔung.
มัน ตัว สูง
4

D Look at the crocodile.

Maa duu sěuua-krôhng.
มา ดู เสือ โคร่ง
5

E The snake is in the tree.

Yàa bpai têe nân.
อย่า ไป ที่ นั่น
6

F Come look at the tiger.

Did you know...?

Horoscopes

The Thai horoscope is very similar to the Chinese horoscope. They both follow the 12 year lunar cycle with each year represented by an animal. However, in the Thai horoscope, the Dragon has been replaced by a Naga. A Naga is a very big snake, like the King Cobra.

Lesson 9 - At Home
Bòttêe 9 - Têe bâahn
บทที่ ๙ – ที่ บ้าน

In this lesson, the student will learn the following:

- Rooms in the house
- Personal pronouns he/she/they
- Activities in the house
- Gamlang (-ing)
- The time of day

Let's follow Kwang's family at home as they get ready to go to school. What do they do after school?

Năi hôrng nám

1 Kim gamlang àab nám.
Kwang gamlang sà pǒm.

Năi hôrng norn

2 Kwang gamlang tàeng tuua.
Ter sài sêua.

Năi hôrng kruua

3 Kim, Cháang láe Kwang gamlang gin kanǒm.
Phûak kǎo gamlang dèuum nom.

Năi hôrng nâng lên

4 Cháang gamlang tham gan bâahn.
Kǎo nèuuay mâak.

Năi hôrng nám

5 Cháang gamlang baaeng fan.
Kim gamlang láang meuuh.

Năi hôrng norn

6 Kim láe Kwang gamlang norn làp.
Phûak ter gamlang fǎn.

Story Translation
Bòd plaae • บท แปล

Mum: Kwang, Kim, tèuun dâi láaew ka!
กวาง, คิม ตื่น ได้ แล้ว ค่ะ
Kwang, Kim, it's time to wake up!

Dad: Cháang, cháo láaew kráp!
ช้าง, เช้า แล้ว ครับ
Chaang, it's morning!

	Năi torn cháo	ใน ตอน เช้า	In the morning

1 | Năi hôrng nám
ห้อง น้ำ
In the bathroom

Kim gamlang **àab nám**.
คิม กำลัง อาบ น้ำ
Kim is **taking a bath**.

Kwang gamlang **sà pǒm**.
กวาง กำลัง สระ ผม
Kwang is **washing her hair**.

2 | Năi hôrng norn
ห้อง นอน
In the bedroom

Kwang gamlang **tàeng tuua**.
กวาง กำลัง แต่ง ตัว
Kwang is **getting dressed**.

Ter **sài** sêua.
เธอ ใส่ เสื้อ
She **puts** on her shirt.

	Năi torn bàai	ใน ตอน บ่าย	In the afternoon

3 | Năi hôrng kruua
ห้อง ครัว
In the kitchen

Kim, Cháang láe Kwang gamlang gin kanǒm.
คิม ช้าง และ กวาง กำลัง กิน ขนม
Kim, Chaang and Kwang are eating a snack.

Phûak kǎo gamlang dèuum nom.
พวก เขา กำลัง ดื่ม นม
They are drinking milk.

4 | Năi hôrng nâng lên
ห้อง นั่ง เล่น
In the living room

Cháang gamlang **tham** gan bâahn.
ช้าง กำลัง ทำ การ บ้าน
Chaang is **doing** his homework.

Kǎo nèuuay mâak.
เขา เหนื่อย มาก
He is very tired.

	Năi torn yen	ใน ตอน เย็น	In the evening

5 | Năi hôrng nám
ห้อง น้ำ
In the bathroom

Cháang gamlang **baaeng fan**.
ช้าง กำลัง แปรง ฟัน
Chaang is **brushing his teeth**.

Kim gamlang **láang meuuh**.
คิม กำลัง ล้าง มือ
Kim is **washing her hands**.

6 | Năi hôrng norn
ห้อง นอน
In the bedroom

Kim láe Kwang gamlang **norn làp**.
คิม และ กวาง กำลัง นอน หลับ
Kim and Kwang are **sleeping**.

Phûak ter gamlang **fǎn**.
พวก เธอ กำลัง ฝัน
They are **dreaming**.

Vocabulary
Kamsàp • คำศัพท์

Àab nám
อาบ น้ำ
To take a bath/shower

Sà pǒm
สระ ผม
To wash your hair

Láang meuuh
ล้าง มือ
To wash your hands

Baaeng fan
แปรง ฟัน
To brush your teeth

Tàeng tuua
แต่ง ตัว
To get dressed

Norn làp
นอน หลับ
To sleep

Fǎn
ฝัน
To dream

Tèuun	ตื่น	To wake up
Torn cháo	ตอน เช้า	Morning
Torn bàai	ตอน บ่าย	Afternoon
Torn yen	ตอน เย็น	Evening
Hôrng	ห้อง	Room
Hôrng nám	ห้อง น้ำ	Bathroom
Hôrng norn	ห้อง นอน	Bedroom
Hôrng kruua	ห้อง ครัว	Kitchen
Hôrng nâng lên	ห้อง นั่ง เล่น	Living room
Ter	เธอ	She
Kǎo	เขา	He/They
Phûak	พวก	Plural article
Sài	ใส่	To put on
Sêua	เสื้อ	Shirt
Nom	นม	Milk
Tham	ทำ	To do
Gan bâahn	การ บ้าน	Homework
Láang	ล้าง	To wash
Meuuh	มือ	Hands
Fan	ฟัน	Teeth

Grammar and language notes
Waiya gawn gàp paa-sǎa • ไวยากรณ์ กับ ภาษา

kǎo — "He" or "they" can be expressed by "kǎo". "Phûak" can be used to emphasise plural.

Kǎo dèuum nom.   **He/they** drink(s) milk.
Phûak kǎo dèuum nom.   **They** drink milk.

gamlang — "Gamlang" expresses a continuous action.

Pǒm **gamlang** lên.   I am play**ing**.
Rao **gamlang** tàeng tuua.   We are gett**ing** dressed.

See Grammar and Language Notes for more details on **personal pronouns** (p.75) and **gamlang** (p.78).

ter — "She" can be expressed by "**ter**".

Ter norn làp.   **She** sleeps.
Ter sà pǒm.   **She** washes her hair.

no possessive pronouns — Unlike English, possessive pronouns are not used in Thai for the following expressions:

Kǎo baaeng fan.   He brushes (his) teeth.
Kǎo sà pǒm.   He washes (his) hair.
Kǎo sài sêua.   He puts on (his) shirt.
Kǎo láang meuuh.   He washes (his) hands.
Kǎo tham gan bâahn.   He does (his) homework.

Exercises
Baaep-fèuk-hàt • แบบ ฝึก หัด

A — Find and circle the words in the grid.

1. Nèuuay — เหนื่อย
2. Fan — ฟัน
3. Gamlang — กำลัง
4. Bâahn — บ้าน
5. Sêua — เสื้อ
6. Dèuum — ดื่ม
7. Phûak — พวก
8. Hôrng nám — ห้อง น้ำ
9. Hôrng kruua — ห้อง ครัว
10. Torn cháo — ตอน เช้า
11. Torn bàai — ตอน บ่าย
12. Torn yen — ตอน เย็น

A	X	W	H	A	V	K	B	F	O	M
B	I	Y	O	N	S	B	A	A	H	N
R	E	H	R	R	D	J	L	N	W	T
H	O	R	N	G	K	R	U	U	A	O
N	Z	J	G	K	L	P	M	I	X	R
E	S	B	N	T	O	R	N	Y	E	N
U	E	G	A	M	L	A	N	G	U	C
U	U	Y	M	K	O	R	N	G	T	H
A	A	N	E	P	H	U	A	K	Y	A
Y	I	Q	V	D	E	U	U	M	B	O
T	O	R	N	B	A	A	I	F	C	Y

B — Is the sentence right or wrong?

Read the following sentences and answer whether they are in the correct room in the house!

> **Examples:**
> Phloi tàeng tuua nǎi hôrng kruua.
> โซฟี ใส่ เสื้อผ้า ใน ห้อง ครัว
> Phloi gets dressed in the kitchen.
> ☐ Right ☑ Wrong
>
> Kǎo gamlang norn nǎi hôrng norn.
> เขา กำลัง นอน ใน ห้อง นอน
> He is sleeping in the bedroom.
> ☑ Right ☐ Wrong

1. Tom àab nám nǎi hôrng kruua.
ทอม อาบ น้ำ ใน ห้อง ครัว
☐ Right ☐ Wrong

2. Phloi baaeng fan nǎi hôrng norn.
โซฟี แปรง ฟัน ใน ห้อง นอน
☐ Right ☐ Wrong

3. Ter sà pǒm nǎi hôrng nám.
เธอ สระ ผม ใน ห้อง น้ำ
☐ Right ☐ Wrong

4. Kǎo láang meuuh nǎi hôrng nâng lên.
เขา ล้าง มือ ใน ห้อง นั่ง เล่น
☐ Right ☐ Wrong

5. Kǎo gin kâao nǎi hôrng krua.
เขา กิน ข้าว ใน ห้อง ครัว
☐ Right ☐ Wrong

6. Tom tham gan bâahn nǎi hôrng nâng lên.
ทอม ทำ การ บ้าน ใน ห้อง นั่ง เล่น
☐ Right ☐ Wrong

Practice speaking Thai by playing the game!

Năi torn cháo	Năi torn bàai	Năi torn yen	Năi hôrng nám	Năi hôrng nâng lên	Năi hôrng norn	Năi hôrng kruua

43	44	45 ?	46 ?	47	48	49 FINISH
42 ?	41	40	39 ?	38	37	36 ?
29	30	31 ?	32 ?	33	34	35
28	27	26	25	24 ?	23	22 ?
15 ?	16	17	18 ?	19	20 ?	21
14	13 ?	12	11	10	9 ?	8
1 START	2	3 ?	4	5	6	7 ?

Instructions:

1. Play the game with one or two other players. The youngest player starts.
2. Roll the dice. If you land on a question mark, you must answer using the clues in the grids according to your position. For instance, if you land on number 9, you must say:
   "**Chăn/Pŏm gamlang norn làp năi hôrng norn ka/kráp.**"
3. The player who cannot answer the question must go back two spaces!
4. The winner of the game is the first player to reach the finish.

PS: Counting must be done in Thai!

D 🖊️ Translate into Thai.

1. I brush my teeth in the morning.

_____

2. I eat a snack in the afternoon.

_____

3. I take a shower in the evening.

_____

4. I wash my hands in the bathroom.

_____

5. They sleep in the bedroom.

_____

6. She does her homework in the living room.

_____

E 🧩 Match and link the Thai words with the English words.

Nǎi hôrng nám
ใน ห้อง น้ำ
1

Ter láang meuuh.
เธอ ล้าง มือ
2

Kǎo yùu nǎi hôrng kruua.
เขา อยู่ ใน ห้อง ครัว
3

Ter dèuum nom.
เธอ ดื่ม นม
4

Kǎo nèuuay.
เขา เหนื่อย
5

Phûak kǎo gamlang norn.
พวก เขา กำลัง นอน
6

A He is tired.

B They are sleeping.

C She drinks milk.

D In the bathroom

E He is in the kitchen.

F She washes her hands.

Did you know...?

Thai Folk Tale

According to a Thai folk tale, some families tell their children the following story:
• In the morning, you should wash your face to wake up.
• In the afternoon, you should wash your upper body to freshen up from the heat.
• Before going to bed, you should wash your feet.
If you go to bed without washing your feet, the angel Tewadaa เทวดา will not be happy!

Lessons 7 - 9 Revision Exercises

A ✏️ **Complete the sentences by choosing a word from the boxes.**

| aàb nám อาบ น้ำ | hôrng kruua ห้อง ครัว | gài satay ไก่ สะเต๊ะ | láe และ | dèuum ดื่ม | nguu งู |

1. Chăn gin _____ ka.　　ฉัน กิน _____ ค่ะ

2. Kwang gamlang _____ năi hôrng nám.　กวาง กำลัง _____ ใน ห้อง น้ำ

3. Kim gamlang gin kanŏm năi _____　คิม กำลัง กิน ขนม ใน _____

4. _____ mee-pit kráp.　　_____ มี พิษ ครับ

5. _____ nám sôm kráp.　　_____ น้ำ ส้ม ครับ

6. Pĕe-sêuua tuua lék _____ sŭuay ka.　ผีเสื้อ ตัว เล็ก _____ สวย ค่ะ

B 🎨 **Draw a picture according to the description below.**

1. Cháang sĕe tao
ช้าง สี เทา

2. Gài satay
ไก่ สะเต๊ะ

3. Nám sôm
น้ำ ส้ม

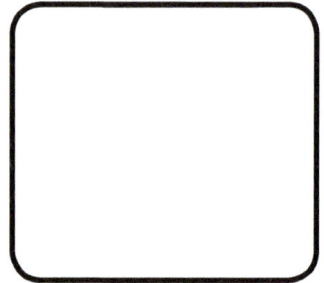

4. Pŏnlamái
ผลไม้

5. Ma-mûuang săm luuk
มะม่วง สาม ลูก

6. Sàparót gàp glûay
สับปะรด กับ กล้วย

7. Jo-ra-kêh sĕe kĕeo
จระเข้ สี เขียว

8. Nguu sĕe lĕuuang
งู สี เหลือง

C ✏️ 👄 Translate the following text in Thai and say it out loud.

Practice ordering food in a restaurant. Translate the sentences below into Thai and repeat them out loud.

1. I would like some rice and chicken satay please.

_____

2. Not spicy please.

_____

3. I would like some orange juice please.

_____

Now, create your own sentence and translate it into Thai.

I would like _____

Chăn/Pŏm kŏr _____

D 🧩 Match and link to the correct response.

Phloi is hungry and thirsty! Match the correct response from her mum when Phloi says "Hĭuw láaew" or "Hĭuw nám".

Her mum's response:

A Aow nám sàparót mái ká?
เอา น้ำ สับปะรด ไหม คะ

Phloi says:

B Aow kâao sŭuay mái ká?
เอา ข้าว สวย ไหม คะ

Hĭuw láaew
หิว แล้ว **1**

C Aow glûay mái ká?
เอา กล้วย ไหม คะ

D Aow nom mái ká?
เอา นม ไหม คะ

E Aow nám ma-mûuang mái ká?
เอา น้ำ มะม่วง ไหม คะ

Hĭuw nám
หิว น้ำ **2**

F Aow kanŏm mái ká?
เอา ขนม ไหม คะ

G Aow nám sôm mái ká?
เอา น้ำ ส้ม ไหม คะ

H Aow gài satay mái ká?
เอา ไก่ สะเต๊ะ ไหม

Create sentences using the following words:

Example: Reuua เรือ - Chăn bpai têe Wat Arun doy **reuua** ka.   ฉัน ไป ที่ วัด อรุณ โดย เรือ ค่ะ

1. Pèt   เผ็ด   _____

2. Sà pǒm   สระ ผม   _____

3. Lék   เล็ก   _____

4. Láang meuuh   ล้าง มือ   _____

5. Hâam   ห้าม   _____

6. Mee-pít   มี พิษ   _____

7. Gin   กิน   _____

8. Yàa   อย่า   _____

9. Nèuuay   เหนื่อย   _____

10. Kanǒm   ขนม   _____

F 🧩 Match and link the activity with the appropriate room in the house.

Activities:

Baaeng fan
แปรง ฟัน **1**

Norn làp
นอน หลับ **2**

Dèuum nom
ดื่ม นม **3**

Láang meuuh
ล้าง มือ **4**

Tàeng tuua
แต่ง ตัว **5**

Aàb nám
อาบ น้ำ **6**

Rooms:

A Hôrng nám
ห้อง น้ำ

B Hôrng norn
ห้อง นอน

C Hôrng kruua
ห้อง ครัว

D Hôrng nâng lên
ห้อง นั่ง เล่น

Grammar and Language Notes

Questions

How to ask and answer a question

To form a direct yes/no question, the word "**mái**" is placed at the end. To say yes in Thai, you sometimes just repeat the verb.

e.g.   Sa-baai dee **mái** kráp?   How are you?*   สบาย ดี ไหม ครับ
       Sa-baai dee ka.   I am well/fine.   สบาย ดี ค่ะ

       Yàak lên dûay gan **mái** ká?   Do you want to play together?   อยาก เล่น ด้วย กัน ไหม คะ
       Yàak kráp!   Yes! ("want!")   อยาก ครับ

* Literally: Are you well?

"**Châi mái?**" can be used when seeking confirmation to the assumption made in the question. The answer is formed using "**châi**" for "**yes**" and "**mâi châi**" for "**no**".

e.g.   Nêe keuu sa-mùd **châi mái** ká?   This is a notebook, isn't it?   นี่ คือ สมุด ใช่ ไหม คะ
       Mâi châi.   **No** it is not.   ไม่ ใช่
       Châi.   **Yes** it is.   ใช่

       Nêe keuu kun yaay **châi mái** ká?   This is your grandmother, isn't it?   นี่ คือ คุณ ยาย ใช่ ไหม คะ
       Mâi châi.   **No** it is not.   ไม่ ใช่
       Châi.   **Yes** it is.   ใช่

Krai (ใคร) Who

Sentences with the question word "**krai**", meaning "**who?**", often follow this pattern: [verb + **krai**?]

The answer can follow this pattern: [(subject) +verb + **answer**]

e.g.   Q: Nân keuu **krai** ká?   **Who** is that?   นั่น คือ ใคร คะ
       A: Nân keuu **kun yaay** ka.   That is my grandmother.   นั่น คือ คุณ ยาย ค่ะ

       Q: Nêe keuu **krai** ká?   **Who** is this?   นี่ คือ ใคร คะ
       A: Nêe keuu **kun dtaa** ka.   This is my grandfather.   นี่ คือ คุณ ตา ค่ะ

Gèe (กี่) How many

Sentences with the question word "**gèe**", meaning "**how many?**", follow this pattern: [subject + verb + noun + **gèe** + classifier]

The answer often follows this structure: [**number** + classifier]

e.g.   Rao mee mà-práaw **gèe** luuk?   **How many** coconuts do we have?   เรา มี มะพร้าว กี่ ลูก
       Jèt luuk.   Seven coconuts.   เจ็ด ลูก

Têe năi (ที่ ไหน) Where

Sentences with the question word "**têe năi**", meaning "**where?**", follow this pattern:

[(subject) + verb + **têe năi**?]

The answers follow this pattern: [(subject) + verb + **têe** + location]

e.g.
Rao yùu **têe năi** ká?	**Where** are we?	เรา อยู่ ที่ ไหน คะ
Rao yùu **têe** Wat Àrun ka.	We are **at** Wat Àrun.	เรา อยู่ ที่ วัด อรุณ ค่ะ
Bpai **têe năi** kráp?	**Where** are you going?	ไป ที่ ไหน ครับ
Bpai **têe** Săo Ching Cháa kráp.	We are going **to** the Giant Swing.	ไป ที่ เสา ชิง ช้า ครับ

Note: The word "**têe**" can be used to express "**to**" or "**at**" but is often omitted in spoken Thai.

A-rai (อะไร) What

Sentences with the question word "**a-rai**", meaning "**what?**" can follow this pattern:

[(subject) + (verb) + **a-rai**?]

The answer can follow this pattern: [(subject) + (verb) + **object**]

e.g.
Nêe keuu **a-rai**?	**What** is this?	นี่ คือ อะไร
Nêe keuu nâng-sĕuu.	This is a book.	นี่ คือ หนังสือ
Keuu **a-rai**?	**What** is it?	คือ อะไร
Din-sŏr.	(It is a) Pencil.	ดินสอ

Note: In spoken Thai, the verb can sometimes be omitted.
e.g.
Nêe a-rai?	What is this?	นี่ อะไร
Nêe din-sŏr.	This is a pencil.	นี่ ดินสอ

Conjunctions & Prepositions

Doy (โดย) By

The word "**by**", indicating the method of going somewhere, can be expressed by the Thai word "**doy**".

Sentences can be constructed as follows: [(subject) + verb + **doy** + transport]

e.g.
Kwang bpai têe wat **doy** reuua.	Kwang goes to the temple **by** boat.	กวาง ไป ที่ วัด โดย เรือ
Kawee bpai têe wat **doy** rót meh.	Kawee goes to the temple **by** bus.	กวี ไป ที่ วัด โดย รถ เมล์

The conjunction "and"

The conjunction "**and**" can be expressed in different ways in Thai. Below are three main forms of the word "**and**":

Gàp (กับ):
"**Gàp**" can be used when enumerating only 2 items. It can also mean "**with**".

e.g.
    Kăo yìp gra-dàat **gàp** gan-grai.
    He takes some paper **and** scissors.
    กาว หยิบ กระดาษ กับ กรรไกร

The conjunction "and" continued...

Láaew-gôr (แล้วก็):

"**Láaew-gôr**" can be used when referring to more than 2 items in a sentence, with "**gàp**" being used to represent the last item.

e.g.   Kăo yìp gra-dàat **láaew-gôr** gan-grai **láaew-gôr** gaao **gàp** năng-sĕuu.
He takes some paper (**and**) scissors (**and**) glue and a book.
กาว หยิบ กระดาษ แล้วก็ กรรไกร แล้วก็ กาว กับ หนังสือ

Láe (และ):

"**Láe**" can be used when describing only one object/person/animal with two expressions.

e.g.   Cháang tuua yài **láe** kăeng-raaeng.   The elephant is big **and** heavy.   ช้าง ตัว ใหญ่ และ แข็ง แรง

Note: When enumerating only 2 items, "**gàp**" or "**láe**" can be used.

Pronouns

Personal Pronouns

There are more personal pronouns in Thai than there are in Western languages. Often, family relationships, social status, female/male, etc. will indicate which personal pronoun to use. Also, personal pronouns can often be omitted in Thai if the context is clear enough. As a base, you should learn the following personal pronouns:

Chăn	I (female speaker)	ฉัน
Pŏm	I (male speaker)	ผม
Kun	You	คุณ
Kăo	He, She, They	เขา
Rao	We	เรา
Man	It	มัน

Notice that "**kăo**" can mean "**he, she or they**". However, you can be more specific.

"**She**" can also be expressed by "**ter**"(เธอ) , especially in written Thai.

e.g.   **Ter** norn làp.   **She** sleeps.   เธอ นอน หลับ
        Ter sà pŏm.   **She** washes her hair.   เธอ สระ ผม

However, "**ter**" can also express "**you**" when combined with "**chăn**" or "**pŏm**".

"**Phûak**" (พวก) can be used with a personal pronoun to explicitly express plural.

e.g.   **Phûak kăo** norn làp.   **They** sleep.   พวก เขา นอน หลับ
        Phûak rao norn làp.   **We** sleep.   พวก เรา นอน หลับ
        Phûak kun norn làp.   **You** sleep.   พวก คุณ นอน หลับ

Expressions without possessive pronouns

Unlike English, possessive pronouns are not used in Thai for the following expressions:

Kăo baaeng fan.	He brushes (his) teeth.	เขา แปรง ฟัน
Kăo sà pŏm.	He washes (his) hair.	เขา สระ ผม
Kăo sài sêua.	He puts on (his) shirt.	เขา ใส่ เสื้อ
Kăo tham gan bâahn.	He does (his) homework.	เขา ทำ การ บ้าน
Kăo láang meuuh.	He washes (his) hands.	เขา ล้าง มือ

The verb "to be"

The verb "**to be**" can be expressed in many different ways. Below are the four main forms of the verb "**to be**":

Keuu (คือ):
"**Keuu**" is used to introduce a person or object.

e.g.   Nân **keuu** kun yaay.   That **is** my grandmother.   นั่น คือ คุณ ยาย
          Nân **keuu** kun mâae.   That **is** my mother.   นั่น คือ คุณ แม่

Yùu (อยู่):
"**Yùu**" is used to describe being physically at a certain location.

e.g.   Kawee **yùu** năi hôrng-reean.   Kawee **is** in the classroom.   กวี อยู่ ใน ห้อง เรียน
          Rao **yùu** têe Wat Àrun.   We **are** at Wat Àrun.   เรา อยู่ ที่ วัด อรุณ

Mee (มี):
"**Mee**" means "**to have**" but can also be used to describe "**there is**" or "**there are**".

e.g.   **Mee** năng-sĕuu nèung lèm.   **There is** one book.   มี หนังสือ หนึ่ง เล่ม
          Mee mà-práaw jèt luuk.   **There are** seven coconuts.   มี มะพร้าว เจ็ด ลูก

Pen (เป็น):
"**Pen**" is used to identify or describe a person (job, nationality, identity, feeling,...) or an object.

e.g.   Pŏm **pen** kon amerigan kráp.   I **am** American.   ผม เป็น คน อเมริกัน ครับ
          Chăn **pen** kon ang-grìt ka.   I **am** English.   ฉัน เป็น คน อังกฤษ ค่ะ

Note: The verb "**to be**" is not used in front of adjectives and adverbs.
e.g.   Plaa sĕe fáa.   The fish (is) blue   ปลา สี ฟ้า
          Kăo reow mâak.   He (is) very fast   เขา เร็ว มาก

Bpai (ไป) To go

The verb "**to go**" can be expressed by using "**bpai**". Sentences can be constructed as follows:

(subject) + **bpai** + (têe) location/verb/etc.

e.g.   Rao **bpai** lên.   We **go** play.   เรา ไป เล่น
          Bpai têe Săo Ching Cháa.   **Go** to the Giant Swing.   ไป ที่ เสา ชิง ช้า

Mee (มี) To have

The verb "**mee**" means "**to have**". It can also mean "**there is/there are**". Sentences often follow this structure:

(subject) + **mee** + noun + number + classifier

e.g.   Chăn **mee** năng-sĕuu nèung lèm.   I **have** one book.   ฉัน มี หนังสือ หนึ่ง เล่ม
          Rao **mee** mà-práaw jèt luuk.   We **have** seven coconuts.   เรา มี มะพร้าว เจ็ด ลูก

The verbs "to like" and "to prefer"

The verb "**to like**" can be expressed by "**châwp**" (ชอบ).

Sentences often follow this structure: (subject) + **châwp** + noun/verb/etc.

e.g. Pŏm **châwp** sĕe daaeng kráp. I **like** red. ผม ชอบ สี แดง ครับ
       Chăn **châwp** plaa ka. I **like** fish. ฉัน ชอบ ปลา ค่ะ

However, the verb "**to prefer**" can be expressed by "**châwp mâak gwàa**" (ชอบ มาก กว่า).

Sentences often follow this structure: (subject) + **châwp** + noun + **mâak gwàa**

e.g. Pŏm **châwp** sĕe fáa **mâak gwàa** kráp. I **prefer** light blue. ผม ชอบ สี ฟ้า มาก กว่า ครับ
       Chăn **châwp** dtào **mâak gwàa** ka. I **prefer** turtles. ฉัน ชอบ เต่า มาก กว่า ค่ะ

The verb "kŏr" (ขอ)

Asking for something in a restaurant, market, shop, etc… can be expressed using the verb "**kŏr**", which can be translated as "….**would like**….".

Sentences often follow this structure: (subject) + **kŏr** + object

e.g. Chăn **kŏr** ma-mûuang ka. I **would like** some mango please. ฉัน ขอ มะม่วง ค่ะ
       Pŏm **kŏr** gài satay kráp. I **would like** chicken satay. ผม ขอ ไก่ สะเต๊ะ ครับ

The verb "aow" (เอา)

Asking someone if she/he wants something can be expressed using the verb "**aow**".

Sentences often follow this structure: (subject) + **aow** + object + **mái?**

e.g. **Aow** nám sôm mái ká? **Would you like** orange juice? เอา น้ำ ส้ม ไหม คะ
       Aow kâao sŭuay mái ká? **Would you like** jasmine rice? เอา ข้าว สวย ไหม คะ

Note: A more formal way of asking "**Would you like…?**" could be done by using the verb "**rap**" (รับ) instead of "**aow**".

The verb "maa" (มา) To come

The verb "**to come**" can be expressed by "**maa**".
Sentences can be constructed as follows: (subject) + **maa** + object/location/etc.

e.g. **Maa** nêe ka. **Come** here. มา นี่ ค่ะ
       Maa duu yee-ráaf ka. **Come** see the giraffe. มา ดู ยีราฟ ค่ะ
       Maa gin kâao ka. **Come** eat. มา กิน ข้าว ค่ะ

Gan tè (กัน เถอะ) Let's

The expression "**let's**" is often expressed in Thai by "**gan tè**" or just "**tè**".

Sentences can be constructed as follows: (subject) + verb + **gan tè**

e.g. Bpai gin **gan tè**. **Let's** go eat. ไป กิน กัน เถอะ
       Bpai lên **gan tè**. **Let's** go play. ไป เล่น กัน เถอะ

Future tense : Jà (จะ) Will

One way of expressing the future tense is to place the word "**jà**" in front of the verb.

Sentences can be constructed as follows: (subject) + **jà** + verb + …

e.g.   Chăn **jà** pûut paa-săa thai ka.   I **will** speak Thai   ฉัน จะ พูด ภาษา ไทย ค่ะ
      Pŏm **jà** bpai têe wat kráp.   I **will** go to the temple.   ผม จะ ไป ที่ วัด ครับ
      Kăo **jà** lên footbawl.   He **will** play football.   เขา จะ เล่น ฟุตบอล

Láaew (แล้ว)

"**Láaew**" is often used to express an action that has already taken place. It can also be used to express the following:

e.g.   Pŏm hĭuw **láaew** kráp.   I am hungry (**already**).   ผม หิว แล้ว ครับ
      Hìm **láaew** kráp.   I am full (**already**).   อิ่ม แล้ว ครับ

Continuous action: Gamlang (กำลัง)

To express an action taking place, the word "**gamlang**" can be used.

Sentences can be constructed as follows: (subject) + **gamlang** + verb + …

e.g.   Pŏm **gamlang** lên kráp.   I am play**ing**.   ผม กำลัง เล่น ครับ
      Rao **gamlang** pûut paa-săa thai.   We are speak**ing** Thai.   เรา กำลัง พูด ภาษา ไทย
      Chăn **gamlang** náp mà-práaw ka.   I am count**ing** coconuts.   ฉัน กำลัง นับ มะพร้าว ค่ะ

Expressions used to forbid certain actions

Negative commands can be expressed by "**Yàa**" or "**Hâam**".

Yàa (อย่า) Do not:
"**Yàa**" is used when ordering someone not to do something. It expresses a strong or urgent command and can be translated by "**Do not**". It is often used by teachers or parents!

e.g.   **Yàa** dèuum!   **Don't** drink!   อย่า ดื่ม
      Yàa bpai!   **Don't** go!   อย่า ไป
      Yàa gin!   **Don't** eat!   อย่า กิน

Hâam (ห้าม) To forbid:
"**Hâam**" is used more as a public order. It is usually seen on public notices and can be translated by "**It is forbidden to …**".

e.g.   **Hâam** jòrt!   **No** stopping!   ห้าม จอด
      Hâam hâi aa-hăan!   **No** feeding!   ห้าม ให้ อาหาร
      Hâam kâo!   **No** entrance!   ห้าม เข้า

Plural

Common nouns in Thai do not vary in order to indicate the plural form. The context usually provides enough information to avoid confusion.

e.g.	Mà-práaw nèung luuk	One coconut	มะพร้าว หนึ่ง ลูก
	Mà-práaw sŏrng luuk	Two coconuts	มะพร้าว สอง ลูก
	Dèk nèung khòn	One child	เด็ก หนึ่ง คน
	Dèk sŏrng khòn	Two children	เด็ก สอง คน

In some cases, you can double a noun to show plural.

e.g.	Dèk	Child	เด็ก
	Dèk dèk	Children	เด็ก ๆ

Classifiers

Classifiers are words used in sentences when enumerating, quantifying or describing a noun. They are necessary in order to speak proper Thai.

Examples of classifiers:

"**khòn**" คน is used with people:	Dèk **khòn** nán	That child	เด็ก คน นั้น
"**tuua**" ตัว is used with animals:	Plaa **tuua** née	This fish	ปลา ตัว นี้
"**luuk**" ลูก is used with round fruits:	Mà-práaw nèung **luuk**	One coconut	มะพร้าว หนึ่ง ลูก
"**lèm**" เล่ม is used with books and magazines:	Năng-sĕuu **lèm** lêhk	A small book	หนังสือ เล่ม เล็ก
"**àn**" อัน is used with miscellaneous or small objects:	Mai-bàn-tat **àn** lêhk	A small ruler	ไม้บรรทัด อัน เล็ก

Classifiers used with adjectives

When using adjectives to describe a noun, the correct classifier needs to be used in the sentence. In the examples below, we are describing animals, for which the classifier is "**tuua**" (ตัว). The classifier will be used for describing size or for counting.

Sentences can be constructed as follows: | Noun + **classifier** + adjective |

e.g.	Yee-ráaf **tuua** sŭung.	The giraffe is tall.	ยีราฟ ตัว สูง
	Cháang **tuua** yài.	The elephant is big.	ช้าง ตัว ใหญ่

However, when describing an animal other than its size, no classifier needs to be used.

e.g.	Yee-ráaf sŭuay.	The giraffe is pretty.	ยีราฟ สวย

Note: The same classifier, **tuua**, can be used when describing the size of a person.

e.g.	Tom **tuua** sŭung	Tom is tall	ทอม ตัว สูง

Numbers

1	nèung	11	sìp et	21	yee sìp et	40	sèe sìp
2	sŏrng	12	sìp sŏrng	22	yee sìp sŏrng	50	hâa sìp
3	săm	13	sìp săm	23	yee sìp săm	60	hòk sìp
4	sèe	14	sìp sèe	24	yee sìp sèe	70	jèt sìp
5	hâa	15	sìp hâa	25	yee sìp hâa	71	jèt sìp et
6	hòk	16	sìp hòk	26	yee sìp hòk	80	bpaaet sìp
7	jèt	17	sìp jèt	27	yee sìp jèt	81	bpaaet sìp et
8	bpaaet	18	sìp bpaaet	28	yee sìp bpaaet	90	gâo sìp
9	gâo	19	sìp gâo	29	yee sìp gâo	91	gâo sìp et
10	sìp	20	yee sìp	30	săm sìp	100	(nèung) rooy

Additional Grammar Notes

Kun (คุณ)

To be more polite, you can add the word "**kun**" in front of mother or father or someone's name.

e.g.
Kun mâae	Mother	คุณ แม่
Kun dam	Dam	คุณ ดำ

Dûay gan (ด้วย กัน)

The Thai expression "**dûay gan**", meaning "**together**", is often used to express an action done with other people. In English, this expression might be omitted.

e.g.
Bpai duu ling **dûay gan**	Go see the monkeys (**together**)	ไป ดู ลิง ด้วย กัน
Bpai lên **dûay gan**	Go play (**together**)	ไป เล่น ด้วย กัน

Sĕe (สี) Colour

The word "**sĕe**" is always displayed before the name of a colour. Without it, you might be saying someone's name!

e.g.
Sĕe dam	Black	สี ดำ
Kun dam	Dam (someone's first name)	คุณ ดำ

Juice

The Thai word "**nám**" (น้ำ) means "**water**". To name any fruit juice or other juice in Thai, follow this pattern:

> **nám** + fruit (or other)

e.g.
Nám sàparót	Pineapple **juice**	น้ำ สับปะรด
Nám sôm	Orange **juice**	น้ำ ส้ม
Nám ma-mûuang	Mango **juice**	น้ำ มะม่วง

No article "a/an" or "the"

In Thai, there is no definite or indefinite article placed in front of a noun. The context makes the meaning clear.

e.g.
Nêe keuu yaang-lóp.	This is (an) eraser.	นี่ คือ ยางลบ
Chăn yìp sa-mùd ka.	I take (the) notebook.	ฉัน หยิบ สมุด ค่ะ

Glossary

A

Aàb nám	อาบ น้ำ	Take a bath/ shower
Aa-hăan	อาหาร	Food
An	อัน	Classifier for misc.objects
Aow	เอา	Would you like?
A-rai	อะไร	What
Aròy	อร่อย	Delicious

B

Baaeng fan	แปรง ฟัน	Brushing teeth
Bâahn	บ้าน	House/home
Bon	บน	On
Bpaaet	แปด	Eight
Bpai	ไป	To go
Bpùu	ปู่	Grandfather

C

Cháa	ช้า	Slow
Chaai hàat	ชาย หาด	Beach
Cháang	ช้าง	Elephant
Châi / Mâi châi	ใช่ / ไม่ ใช่	Yes/No
Chăn	ฉัน	I (female speaker)
Châwp	ชอบ	To like
Châwp mâak gwàa	ชอบ มาก กว่า	To prefer
Chêuu	ชื่อ	Name

D

Dèk dèk	เด็กๆ	Children
Dèk	เด็ก	Child
Derrn	เดิน	Walking
Derrn bpai	เดิน ไป	Go walking
Dèuum	ดื่ม	To drink
Din-sŏr sĕe	ดินสอ สี	Crayons
Din-sŏr	ดินสอ	Pencil
Doy	โดย	By
Dtaa	ตา	Grandfather
Dtào	เต่า	Turtle
Dûay gan	ด้วย กัน	Together
Duu	ดู	To look

F

Făn	ฝัน	Dreaming
Fan	ฟัน	Teeth

G

Gaao	กาว	Glue
Gài satay	ไก่ สะเต๊ะ	Chicken satay
Gài	ไก่	Chicken
Gamlang	กำลัง	-ing ending
Gan bâahn	การ บ้าน	Homework
Gan tè	กัน เถอะ	Let's...
Gan-grai	กรรไกร	Scissors
Gâo	เก้า	Nine
Gàp	กับ	And
Gèe	กี่	How many
Gèng mâak	เก่ง มาก	Well done
Gin	กิน	To eat
Glàp	กลับ	Go back/return
Glûay	กล้วย	Banana
Gra-dàat	กระดาษ	Paper

H

Hâa	ห้า	Five
Hâam	ห้าม	Forbidden to...
Hâi aa-hăan	ให้ อาหาร	To feed
Hìm láaew	อิ่ม แล้ว	To be full
Hĭuw láaew	หิว แล้ว	To be hungry
Hĭuw nám	หิว น้ำ แล้ว	To be thirsty
Hòk	หก	Six
Hông kruua	ห้อง ครัว	Kitchen
Hông nám	ห้อง น้ำ	Bathroom
Hông nâng lên	ห้อง นั่ง เล่น	Living room
Hông norn	ห้อง นอน	Bedroom
Hông	ห้อง	Room
Hông-reean	ห้อง เรียน	Classroom

J

Jà	จะ	Will
Jàkgrayaan	จักรยาน	Bicycle
Jap	จับ	To touch
Jèt	เจ็ด	Seven
Jing jing	จริงๆ	Really
Jo-ra-kêh	จระเข้	Crocodiles
Jòrt	จอด	Stop

K

Ka	ค่ะ	Polite article
Kâao	ข้าว	Rice
Kâao pad	ข้าว ผัด	Fried rice
Kăeng-raaeng	แข็ง แรง	Heavy
Kanŏm	ขนม	Dessert (or snack)
Kăo	เขา	He/They
Kâo	เข้า	Entry/to enter
Kao-rób	เคารพ	Pay respect
Keuu	คือ	To be
Khan	คัน	Classifier for cars
Khòn	คน	Classifier for people

Kilo	กิโล	Kilo
Klaan	คลาน	To crawl
Kŏr	ขอ	Would like…
Korpkun	ขอบคุณ	Thank you
Krai	ใคร	Who
Kráp	ครับ	Polite article
Krêuang bin	เครื่อง บิน	Airplane
Kropkruua	ครอบครัว	Family
Kun kruu	คุณ ครู	Teacher
Kun	คุณ	A person
Kun	คุณ	You
Kwaay	ควาย	Water buffalo

L

Là	ล่ะ	What about
Láaew	แล้ว	Past tense
Láaew-gôr	แล้วก็	And
Láang	ล้าง	To wash
Láang meuuh	ล้าง มือ	Washing hands
Láe	และ	And
Lêhk	เลข	Number
Lék	เล็ก	Small
Lèm	เล่ม	Classifier for books
Lên	เล่น	To play
Léuuay	เลื้อย	To crawl
Ling	ลิง	Monkey
Luuk	ลูก	Son or daughter
Luuk	ลูก	Classifier for round fruits

M

Maa	มา	To come
Măa	หมา	Dog
Mâae	แม่	Mother
Maaew	แมว	Cat
Mâak	มาก	Very
Mái	ไหม	Question word
Mâi	ไม่	No, not
Mái-ban-tát	ไม้บรรทัด	Ruler
Malagor	มะละกอ	Papaya
Ma-mûuang	มะม่วง	Mango
Man	มัน	It
Mà-práaw	มะพร้าว	Coconut
Mee	มี	To have
Mee-pít	มี พิษ	Poisonous
Meuuh	มือ	Hands

N

Nà	นะ	Polite form
Nâa gluua	น่า กลัว	Frightening
Năi	ใน	In
Nák-reean	นักเรียน	Student
Nám sôm	น้ำ ส้ม	Orange juice
Nám	น้ำ	Water

Nân	นั่น	That
Nán	นั้น	That!
Nâng Long	นั่ง ลง	Sit down
Năng-sĕuu	หนังสือ	Book
Náp	นับ	To count
Née	นี้	This!
Nêe	นี่	This
Nèung	หนึ่ง	One
Nèuuay	เหนื่อย	Tired
Ngau	เงาะ	Rambutan
Nguu	งู	Snake
Nít nòy	นิด หน่อย	A little bit
Nom	นม	Milk
Nóng săo	น้องสาว	Little sister
Norn làp	นอน หลับ	To sleep

P

Paa-să	ภาษา	Language
Pàk	ผัก	Vegetables
Pêe chaay	พี่ชาย	Big brother
Pêe-sêuua	ผีเสื้อ	Butterfly
Pèt	เผ็ด	Spicy
Pêuuan	เพื่อน	Friend
Phûak	พวก	Plural article
Pipittapan sàtnám	พิพิธภัณฑ์ สัตว์น้ำ	Aquarium
Plaa chà-lăm	ปลา ฉลาม	Shark
Plaa	ปลา	Fish
Pô	พ่อ	Father
Pŏm	ผม	I
Pŏnlamái	ผลไม้	Fruits
Pûut	พูด	Speak

R

Rao	เรา	We
Reean	เรียน	To study
Reow	เร็ว	Fast
Reuua	เรือ	Boat
Rót faifáa	รถ ไฟฟ้า	Electric train
Rót jàkgrayaan yòn	รถ จักรยาน ยนต์	Motocycle
Rót meh	รถเมล์	Bus
Rót taxi	รถ แท็กซี่	Taxi
Rót túk túk	รถ ตุ๊กตุ๊ก	Tuk tuk
Rót yon	รถ ยนต์	Car

S

Sà pŏm	สระ ผม	Washing hair
Sa-baai dee	สบาย ดี	To be fine
Sài	ใส่	To put on
Săm	สาม	Three
Sa-mùd	สมุด	Notebook
Sànuk	สนุก	Having fun
Sàparót	สับปะรด	Pineapple
Sà-thănee	สถานี	Station

Sà-wàtdee	สวัสดี	Hello/Goodbye
Sĕe chompuu	สี ชมพู	Pink
Sĕe daaeng	สี แดง	Red
Sĕe dam	สี ดำ	Black
Sĕe fáa	สี ฟ้า	Light blue
Sĕe kăaw	สี ขาว	White
Sĕe kĕeo	สี เขียว	Green
Sĕe lĕuuang	สี เหลือง	Yellow
Sĕe mûuang	สี ม่วง	Purple
Sĕe nám ngen	สี น้ำ เงิน	Dark blue
Sĕe nám taan	สี น้ำตาล	Brown
Sĕe sôm	สี ส้ม	Orange
Sĕe tao	สี เทา	Grey
Sèe	สี่	Four
Sêua	เสื้อ	Shirt
Sĕuua-krôhng	เสื้อ โคร่ง	Tiger
Sìp	สิบ	Ten
Sôm	ส้ม	Orange
Sŏrng	สอง	Two
Sŭan-sàt	สวน สัตว์	Zoo
Sŭuay	สวย	Pretty
Sŭung	สูง	Tall

T

Tàeng tuua	แต่ง ตัว	To get dressed
Ta-gohn	ตะโกน	To shout
Tâi	ใต้	Under
Tàlàat	ตลาด	Market
Têe năi	ที่ ไหน	Where
Têe nêe	ที่ นี่	Here

Têe sùt	ที่ สุด	The most
Têe	ที่	At/To
Ter	เธอ	She/You
Tèuun	ตื่น	To wake up
Thai	ไทย	Thai
Tham	ทำ	To do
Tônmái	ต้นไม้	Tree
Tôn mà-práaw	ต้น มะพร้าว	Coconut tree
Tòr	ต่อ	Next
Torn bàai	ตอน บ่าย	Afternoon
Torn cháo	ตอน เช้า	Morning
Torn yen	ตอน เย็น	Evening
Tuua	ตัว	Classifier

W

Wâay	ว่าย	To swim
Wannée	วันนี้	Today
Wat	วัด	Temple

Y

Yâa	ย่า	Grandmother
Yàa	อย่า	Do not ....
Yàak	อยาก	To want
Yaang-lóp	ยางลบ	Eraser
Yaaw	ยาว	Long
Yaay	ยาย	Grandmother
Yài	ใหญ่	Big
Yee-ráaf	ยีราฟ	Giraffe
Yìp	หยิบ	To take
Yùu	อยู่	To be

Keys to Exercises

Lesson 1

(A) 1. ka 2. chêuu 3.ka 4. mái 5. kráp. 6. Chǎn

(B) 1C 2D 3E 4B 5F 6A

(D) 1. Sà-wàtdee ka/kráp.
2. Kun chêuu a-rai ká/kráp?
3. Pǒm chêuu Kawee kráp.
4. Sa-baai dee mái ká/kráp?
5. Sa-baai dee ka/kráp. Kun là ká/kráp?

(E)

P	C	V	T	I	Y	C	H	A	N
O	A	D	K	A	T	L	R	R	V
M	R	L	V	R	C	E	F	K	P
X	S	A	W	A	T	D	E	E	X
M	F	J	P	I	R	Z	Q	P	D
L	X	U	K	O	R	P	K	U	N
B	K	P	M	I	U	N	E	F	H
F	R	J	K	S	C	H	E	U	U
M	A	I	U	X	P	S	H	B	E
W	P	X	N	G	E	I	A	U	P

Lesson 2

(A) 1. Yes 2. No 3. No 4. Yes

(B) 1D 2F 3A 4B 5C 6E

(C) 1. Nêe keuu krai ká?
2. Sànuk mái ká?
3. Nêe keuu kun mâae.
4. Kun dtaa/kun bpùu
5. Nêe keuu pêe chaay.
6. Kataleeya gàp Kwang lên dûay gan.

(D) 1. mái 2. krai 3. keuu 4. gàp 5. lên

Lesson 3

(A) 1. Kawee bpai têe bâahn doy rót túk túk.
2. Rao yùu têe tàlàat nát Jà-tù-jàk.
3. Kwang bpai têe tàlàat doy rót meh.
4. Rao yùu têe nǎi ká/kráp?
5. Rao jà bpai têe nǎi ká/ kráp?
6. Rao derrn bpai têe bâahn

(B) 1. Derrn   4. Rót taxi   7. Rót meh
2. Rót túk túk   5. Reuua   8. Rót yon
3. Rót faifáa   6. Krêuang bin 9. Jàkgrayaan

(D) List 1 - A   List 2 - B   List 3 - C

(E) 1F 2E 3A 4C 5D 6B

Revision Exercises 1-3

(A) 1. Reuua 2. Chêuu 3. Kun yaay 4.Pǒm 5.Yùu 6.Doy

(B) 1. Sà-wàtdee ka/kráp. Chǎn/ Pǒm chêuu [name] ka/kráp.
2. Kun chêuu a-rai ká/kráp?
3. Pǒm chêuu Kawee kráp.
4. Sabai dee ka/kráp, korpkun ka/kráp.

(C) 1. Electric train 4. Car   7. Walk/walking
2. Grandfather   5. Older brother 8. Mum
3. Boat   6. Plane

(D) A 1. Sabai dee mái kráp?
2. Sànuk mái ká?
3. Kawee glàp bâahn mái ká?
4. Yàak lên dûay gan mái kráp?

B 1. Kun pô yùu têe nǎi ká?
2. Kawee yùu têe nǎi ká?
3. Rao yùu têe nǎi ká?
4. Kwang jà bpai têe nǎi kráp?

C 1. Nân keuu krai ká?
2. Nân keuu krai ká?
3. Nêe keuu krai kráp?
4. Nêe keuu krai kráp?

(E) 1. Mum   5. At/to   9. I (female)
2. What   6. Bus   10. Temple
3. Name   7. Where
4. Go   8. We

(F) 1F 2H 3D 4J 5A 6C 7I 8E 9B 10G

Lesson 4

(A) A3 B5 C10 D9 E7 F6 G4 H8 I2 J1

(B) 1. Five children   3. Six coconut trees
2. Eight monkeys   4. Four coconuts

(C) 1F 2E 3C 4B 5A 6D

(D) 1. sǒrng 2. sìp 3. hâa 4. sǎm 5. gâo 6. jèt

(E) 1. Mà-práaw bpaaet luuk
2. Wannée rao jà tham a-rai dee kráp/ká?
3. Bpai
4. Rao mee ling gèe tuua kráp/ká?
5. Ling sìp tuua
6. Rao mee mà-práaw luuk hâa.

Lesson 5

(A) 1. Sěe daaeng   4. Sěe nám taan   7. Sěe lěuuang
2. Sěe chompuu   5. Sěe tao   8. Sěe mûuang
3. Sěe fáa   6. Sěe dam   9. Sěe kěeo

(B) List 1 - B   List 2 - C   List 3 - A   List 4 - B

(C) 1C   2F   3A   4B   5D   6E

(D)

(E) 1. Plaa sĕe sôm gàp sĕe kăaw.
2. Pŏm/chăn châwp sĕe dam gàp sĕe lĕuuang kráp/ka.
3. Dtào sĕe kĕeo.
4. Plaa chà-lăm sĕe tao.
5. Rao jà bpai têe pipíttapan sàtnám ka/kráp.
6. Pŏm/chăn châwp sĕe daaeng mâak gwàa kráp/ka.

Lesson 6

(A) 1C   2E   3D   4A   5F   6B

(B) 1. Sa-mùd   3. Gra-dàat   5. Din-sŏr
2. Gan-grai   4. Năng-sĕuu   6. Yaang-lóp

(C) 1. Nâng long ka/kráp.
2. Gèng mâak, nák-reean.
3. Yìp mái-ban-tát nà ká/kráp.
4. Nêe keuu din-sŏr sĕe châi mái kráp/ká?
5. Nêe keuu din-sŏr kráp/ka.
6. Nân keuu din-sŏr kráp/ka.

(D) 1. Châi ka. Nêe keuu gra-dàat ka.
2. Châi ka. Nêe keuu năng-sĕuu ka.
3. Mâi châi ka. Nêe keuu din-sŏr ka.
4. Mâi châi ka. Nêe keuu gan-grai ka.
5. Châi ka. Nêe keuu din-sŏr sĕe ka.
6. Mâi châi ka. Nêe keuu mái-ban-tát ka.

(E) 1. Gan-grai   4. Gaao   7. Yaang-lóp
2. Kun kruu   5. Nak-reean   8. Gra-dàat
3. Mái-ban-tát   6. Sa-mùd   9. Năng-sĕuu

Revision Exercises 4-6

(A) 1. sìp   3. kĕeo   5. paa-săa
2. sĕe daaeng   4. nák-reean   6. hâa

(B) 1. tuua   Three fish
2. lèm   Eight books
3. khòn   Four children
4. luuk   Five coconuts
5. tuua   One turtle
6. khòn   Seven friends
7. lèm   Nine notebooks
8. lèm   Two scissors
9. àn   Six erasers
10. àn   Ten rulers

(C) 1. Bpaaet lèm ka.   4. Sŏrng tuua ka.
2. Hâa khòn kráp.   5. Sèe tuua kráp.
3. Săm tuua ka.   6. Hòk lèm ka.

(D) 1. Six   5. Thai language   9. Classroom
2. To like   6. Today   10. To have
3. Light blue   7. Orange (color)
4. Teacher   8. Ten

(E) 1. Crayons   4. Brown monkey   7. Pink ruler
2. Green turtle   5. Black book   8. Three
3. Red fish   6. Scissors and glue   coconuts.

(F) 1. Nêe keuu gra-dàat ka.
2 Nêe keuu din-sŏr sĕe ka.
3. Nêe keuu năng-sĕuu ka.
4. Nêe keuu mái-ban-tát ka.
5. Nêe keuu sa-mùd ka.
6. Nêe keuu din-sŏr ka.

Lesson 7

(A) 1D   2F   3E   4A   5B   6C

(B) 1. Phloi hĭuw nám.
2. Kwang hĭuw láaew
3. Tom hìm láaew
4. Gin a-rai kráp/ká?
5. Aròy
6. Pŏm/chăn châwp nám ma-mûuang kráp/ka.

(C)

A	B	W	U	G	I	N	B	P	A	T	H
D	E	U	U	M	X	K	X	E	R	Y	Q
R	N	H	F	R	K	J	L	T	P	X	J
P	O	N	L	A	M	A	I	J	V	L	C
B	Z	I	C	V	L	P	M	K	A	A	O
A	R	T	V	Q	K	X	T	D	P	O	S
R	L	N	D	T	G	B	H	I	E	W	L
O	N	O	S	K	O	R	N	R	G	E	T
Y	G	Y	E	O	F	H	X	K	I	L	O

(D) 1. Orange (fruit)   3. Dessert   5. Chicken
2. Pineapple   4. Vegetable

Lesson 8

(A) 1. Pĕe-sêuua   4. Cháang   7. Nguu
2. Jo-ra-kêh   5. Kwaay
3. Yee-ráaf   6. Sĕuua-krôhng

(B) 1. Yee-ráaf tuua sŭung.
2. Pĕe-sêuua tuua lék.
3. Sĕuua-krôhng tuua yài.
4. Jo-ra-kêh nâa-gluua.
5. Cháang tuua yài.
6. Kwaay tuua kăeng-raaeng.

(C) 1. Little elephant   3. Pretty butterfly
2. Big elephant   4. Scary butterfly!

(D) 1. Jo-ra-kêh   3. Hâam   5. Mee-pít
2. Sŭuay   4. Duu   6. Yàa

(E) 1D   2E   3A   4B   5F   6C

Lesson 9

(A)

A	X	W	H	A	V	K	B	F	O	M
B	I	Y	O	N	S	B	A	A	H	N
R	E	H	R	R	D	J	L	N	W	T
H	O	R	N	G	K	R	U	U	A	O
N	Z	J	G	K	L	P	M	I	X	R
E	S	B	N	T	O	R	N	Y	E	N
U	E	G	A	M	L	A	N	G	U	C
U	U	Y	M	K	O	R	N	G	T	H
A	A	N	E	P	H	U	A	K	Y	A
Y	I	Q	V	D	E	U	U	M	B	O
T	O	R	N	B	A	A	I	F	C	Y

(B) 1. Wrong 2. Wrong 3. Right 4. Wrong 5. Right 6. Right

(D)
1. Pŏm/chăn baaeng fan năi torn cháo kráp/ka.
2. Pŏm/chăn gin kanom năi torn bài kráp/ka.
3. Pŏm/chăn àab nám năi torn yen kráp/ka .
4. Pŏm/chăn láang meuuh năi hôrng nám kráp/ka.
5. Phûak kăo norn làp năi hôrng norn.
6. Ter tham gan bâahn năi hôrng nâng lên

(E) 1D 2F 3E 4C 5A 6B

Revision Exercises 7-9

(A)
1. Gài satay   3. Hôrng kruua   5. Dèuum
2. Aab nám   4. Nguu   6. Láe

(B)
1. A grey elephant   5. Three mangoes
2. Chicken satay   6. A pineapple and a banana
3. Orange juice   7. A green crocodile
4. Fruits   8. A yellow snake

(C)
1. Pŏm/chăn kŏr kâao gàp gài satay kráp/ka.
2. Mâi pèt kráp/ka.
3. Pŏm/chăn kŏr nám sôm kráp/ka.

(D) 1 - BCFH   2 - ADEG

(E)
1. Spicy   5. No…(forbidden..)   9. Tired
2. To wash hair   6. Poisonous   10. Dessert
3. Small   7. To eat
4. To wash hands   8. Do not….

(F) 1A 2B 3C 4A or C 5B 6A

Contributors' Biographies

Karine Jones คารีน โจนส์

Karine was born and raised in Belgium. She attended university in the US and later in Belgium where she graduated with a BA. She also has an MBA from Heriot Watt University, Edinburgh. She has lived and worked in many countries, including Japan, Luxembourg and the USA among others. Being multilingual, she has always been interested in foreign languages. Since adopting their son from Thailand, Karine has been fascinated with the Thai language and culture. She presently lives in the United Kingdom with her husband and her young son.

Jessica Emmett เจสสิก้า เอ็มเมตต์

Jessica is a Vietnamese adoptee born and raised in Hong Kong by British parents. She then moved to the UK with her family at the age of 16. She has a BA in Photography and a MA (with distinction) in Media Arts from Manchester Metropolitan University, UK. Since leaving university she has been working as a freelance artist, illustrator & designer. As well as her general freelance work, she often works in collaboration with people that have a connection with (transracial) adoption. To see more of her work visit: www.jessica-emmett.com

Onanong Wongprasert อรอนงค์ วงษ์ประเสริฐ

Kwang was born and raised in Thailand. She has a BA in Thai language from Srinakharinwirot University, Bangkok and an MA in Education: Culture, Language and Identity from Goldsmiths University of London, UK. She has extensive experience teaching Thai as a foreign language, both at schools and as a private tutor. Kwang is passionate about teaching Thai. She believes it helps to promote Thai culture and brings people closer together.

Notes

Notes